At Issue

| Should the United States
Be Multilingual?

Other Books in the At Issue Series:

At Issue

Should the United States Be Multilingual?

Amy Francis, Book Editor

GREENHAVEN PRESS
A part of Gale, Cengage Learning

Detroit • New York • San Francisco • New Haven, Conn • Waterville, Maine • London

Christine Nasso, *Publisher*
Elizabeth Des Chenes, *Managing Editor*

© 2011 Greenhaven Press, a part of Gale, Cengage Learning.

Gale and Greenhaven Press are registered trademarks used herein under license.

For more information, contact:
Greenhaven Press
27500 Drake Rd.
Farmington Hills, MI 48331-3535
Or you can visit our Internet site at www.gale.cengage.com

For product information and technology assistance, contact us at

Gale Customer Support, 1-800-877-4253
For permission to use material from this text or product, submit all requests online at www.cengage.com/permissions

Further permissions questions can be e-mailed to permissionrequest@cengage.com

Articles in Greenhaven Press anthologies are often edited for length to meet page requirements. In addition, original titles of these works are changed to clearly present the main thesis and to explicitly indicate the author's opinion. Every effort is made to ensure that Greenhaven Press accurately reflects the original intent of the authors. Every effort has been made to trace the owners of copyrighted material.

Cover image © Images.com/Corbis.

LIBRARY OF CONGRESS CATALOGING-IN-PUBLICATION DATA

Should the United States be multilingual? / Amy Francis, book editor.
    p. cm. -- (At issue)
Includes bibliographical references and index.
ISBN 978-0-7377-4892-5 -- ISBN 978-0-7377-4893-2 (pbk.)
1. Language policy--United States. 2. Language planning--United States. 3. Multilingualism--United States. 4. Bilingual education--United States. I. Francis, Amy.
    P119.32.U6.S56 2011
    306.44'973--dc22

                                                                2010037586

Printed in the United States of America
1 2 3 4 5 6 7 14 13 12 11 10

Contents

Introduction

Most media coverage surrounding multilingualism focuses on recent immigrants learning English as a second language. Likewise, bilingual education generally refers to educating non-English speaking students within the public school system with the goal of English proficiency. Thus, multilingualism often is a contentious topic discussed alongside immigration, racism, minority rights, and national language.

It is certainly true that learning English is a major issue in the United States. According to the U.S. Department of Education's Office of Vocational and Adult Education, Division of Adult Education and Literacy, 1,172,569 adults were enrolled in state-administered English language programs during 2003–2004. Additionally, as reported by the Office of English Language Acquisition, approximately 5,074,572 children with limited English proficiency were enrolled in grades pre-Kindergarten through twelve during the 2005–2006 school year. However, English is not the only second language Americans are learning. The reasons people choose to learn a second language are as diverse as the people seeking to become multilingual.

According to the National Center for Family Literacy and the Center for Applied Linguistics, people may enroll in an English-language program not only "to improve English proficiency, but also to get a better job, complete a high school diploma or higher education degree, support their candidacy for American citizenship, and develop skills that will help their own children succeed academically." Likewise, many English-speaking adults seek to learn a second language for similar reasons, and the market for educational materials in many languages is booming. According to Kendall King and Lyn Fogle of Georgetown University, writing for the Center for Applied Linguistics, "The reasons for this trend include a desire to maintain ties to the parents' heritage, language, and culture; to provide children with academic and cognitive advantages; and to promote cross-cultural understanding and communication." In addition to helping children achieve academically, there may be other benefits for bilingual adults as well. A 2006 Canadian study as reported in the *Globe and Mail* (Toronto), found that knowing multiple languages could delay the onset of dementia.

Whatever the reasons a person has for desiring to acquire a second language, the questions of how to best learn and when, continue to be the topic of much research. Generally it is accepted that children have an easier time learning a second language, so many parents seek to introduce their children to a second language as early as possible.

Christina Bosemark, mother of two multilingual children and the founder of the Multilingual Children's Association, writes that "there are a multitude of strategies for raising bilingual children." She points out however, "Studies indicate that children need exposure to a different language about one-third of their waking hours to become actively bilingual. They'll likely understand a lot with less interaction, but they probably won't be able to speak it themselves. Learning a language is simple for children, relative to adults, but in the beginning they actually need to hear a word thousands of times before it sticks."

As explained by Bosemark, a couple of common methods for teaching children a second language include "One Parent, One Language," also known as OPOL, and Minority Language at Home. With OPOL, each parent consistently speaks to the child in only one language. With Minority Language at Home, the entire family commits to speaking the minority language at home at all times. Parents often wonder, however, how to help their child become bilingual if they themselves are not fluent in a second language. One option is to seek out an education for their child at a school that teaches in another language. For example, in Montreal, Canada, the method used to teach French to English-speaking children is to start school entirely in French. This method has become the example for many other schools around the world.

Two-way immersion programs, also known as dual-language programs, also are gaining popularity as a way to teach children a second language. These programs begin early—usually in first or second grade. In this program half the students are fluent in English and the other half are fluent in a second language, typically Spanish. The goal is to promote language development, with both groups of students having a chance to be the language modelers and the language learners, as well as to promote greater cross-cultural understanding.

Most researchers agree that the easiest way to acquire a second language is by full immersion, either in the culture where the language is spoken, at home, or in school. Dr. Christina Schelletter, a senior lecturer in English Language and Communication in the School of Humanities at the University of Hertfordshire, leads a United Kingdom-based language investigation. She stated in *ScienceDaily* on September 10, 2009, "We have found that immersion-type teaching can be of real benefit to children. Immersion is the best and most successful method of foreign language learning at an early age. The natural learning abilities of young children as well as their enthusiasm promise rapid and successful acquisition of the second language."

What if a person did not learn a second language as a child, however, and he or she would like to become bilingual as an adult? Many people believe learning is more difficult for adults, but new research shows that acquiring a second language in adulthood may not be as difficult as previously believed. As reported in a June 15, 2005, *ScienceDaily* article, Dr. Paul Iverson of University College London's Centre for Human Communication found that just because someone did not learn a second language during childhood, does not mean he or she has lost the opportunity to become bilingual. Iverson states, "We change our perception during childhood so that it becomes specialized to hear the speech sounds in our first language. This specialization can conflict with our ability to learn to distinguish sounds in other languages. Through training, we can essentially change our 'perceptual warping' to make second-language learning easier. I hope that this research will lead to new ways of training adults to learn second languages." There are numerous options for adults who desire to learn a second language, including through conversation groups as well as classes at community centers, libraries, and local colleges.

Aside from the challenges faced by those learning a second language, numerous other language considerations continue to be hotly debated, including whether the United States should have an official language and the potential value of being a multilingual nation. *At Issue: Should the United States Be Multilingual?* explores these and other issues.

1

English Should Be the National Language of the United States

Steve King

Steve King was elected to Congress in 2002 to represent Iowa's fifth congressional district. He also is a member of the House Judiciary Committee where he serves on both the Constitution Subcommittee and the Immigration Subcommittee.

A common language unites Americans by enabling communication in business, legal documents, and global affairs. Further, because English is used around the world, establishing it as the national language would give the United States an advantage over countries where English is not the primary language. Immigrants may fear losing their culture if they learn English, but learning English will greatly benefit immigrants by giving them better opportunities. Accepting English as the official language would be a giant step toward encouraging immigrants to learn this valuable language and toward maintaining the unity of our country.

There is something unique about being an American. It is something unique, that it is different than coming from another nation in the world. We brought together all people from all cultures and all civilizations and assimilated them into this society to produce a common culture, a form of cultural continuity that binds us together as Americans.

As I listen and engage in debate, and as I read and study history and watch the reactions of people around me and

Steve King, "Promoting the English Unity Act," *Congressional Record*, December 6, 2007.

think what it must have been like 50 years ago, when I wasn't quite paying attention in this country, or 100 years ago, when I wasn't around, or 200 years ago obviously, as America was shaped, what is it that is unique about us? What has given us our vitality? What has bound us together so that we can work together as one people?

There are a number of common denominators. We live in the same geographical area, we share a common history and we adhere to the rule of law. English common law flowed across the Atlantic Ocean and was established here in this continent, actually not too far down the coastline down at Jamestown in 1607 in Virginia. Four hundred years ago English common law arrived here in the United States.

A Common Language Binds Us Together

But another thing that has taken place that is a common denominator, that has bound us together, that has been a powerful force for our society, for the American interests, and a powerful force throughout all humanity, is to have a common language.

Now, one can just take the globe at about any time, and let's just say going backwards across history, generation by generation, recognizing that national boundaries have shifted over time. They shift because of political transformations within the countries and they shift because of wars.

A common language has defined the boundaries of nation-states throughout history.

You can take this back to the city-state era before we actually had nation-states, and identify that the boundaries around the city-states and the boundaries around the nation-states from 300 years ago and earlier were often boundaries that were drawn by lines of language.

Languages grew up in colloquial regions, and because people communicated with each other verbally, languages evolved. And because people didn't travel in those days the way they travel today, then the languages that evolved in certain locales got more and more distinct and more difficult for the neighbors to understand.

Of course, we track language through, and because of commonalities in language, we also track the migrations and histories of people. But a common language has defined the boundaries of nation-states throughout history.

In France, they speak French; in England, they speak English; in Spain, they speak Spanish; in Portugal, they speak Portuguese; in China they speak Chinese; in Russia, they speak Russian. Why is that? I never hear anybody talk about that. But the reason for that is because of common languages, the languages have defined the boundaries of nations, of nation-states.

Why does a nation-state have a boundary that is defined by its languages? It is because they are a common people. Whether they are Italians or Spaniards or French, they are a common people that are bound together by a common language. They have a common cause. They have a common sense of history. They work together. They communicate with each other. They do business together with far less suspicion because they can communicate quickly and effectively and efficiently with a common language. . . .

English Gives the United States a Global Advantage

English was the language that was the language of our original settlers here in the largest number. It could have been German, it could have been French, it could have been Spanish. You can make a case for that throughout history.

There is no case that I can think of to be made for the official language of the United States being anything else other than English.

But whatever that case is, it is English today. And English happens to be also the global language of commerce. It is the language we do business in in the world. It is the language that we negotiate politically in. At the roundtable in Brussels [Belgium], at the European Union, when we sit around that roundtable and negotiate with all of those member nations, now I can't actually keep track, it was 15 when I was there last, I think it has gone to 25. But the language of negotiations in Europe around the roundtable at Brussels in the European Union is English. The representatives there, the French speak English, the Spanish speak English, the Portuguese speak English, because there needs to be a common language of communication. What will it be?

What will the documents be printed in? Do they get printed in 300-some languages that we commonly talk of as being the utilized number of languages in the globe? Or can it be printed in one? Well, if you have a common language, one is it. There is only one definition, there is only one understanding, and there is no misunderstanding, at least substantially less misunderstanding, excuse me.

So if a common language, an official language, a language of communications at the European Union in Brussels is English, and if the international language of business and commerce is English, and it is, and the international language of air traffic controllers that commands all airplanes that are flying and being controlled by air traffic controllers in America is English, and it is, and if the language of the maritime industry, the language that tells ships how to avoid running into each other in the fog is English, and English is the common language of the United States of America, and it gives us a competitive advantage with the rest of the world that does not speak English as fluently when it comes to business, and if it is the language we use when we negotiate in our trade relationships with other countries and the language we use when we negotiate our political disagreements and arrive at our agreements is English, then there is no case that I can think of to be made for the official language of the United States being anything else other than English. . . .

The Problem of Being Multilingual

So when we talk about establishing an official language here, English, the official language of the United States, and I hear people cry out that somehow that is a major inconvenience to people who come here speaking other languages and that we don't need an official language, that kind of argument defies the logic of the rest of the world. The logic of the rest of the world understands that there has to be official documents, there have to be official proceedings. There has to be an agreement on what language means. And if we will accept any language into our official activities here in the Federal Government, then we are forever litigating the differences between the interpretations of those languages.

For example, let's just say that we had two people that came together and signed a contract, and one of them wanted that contract in Vietnamese and the other wanted the contract in Korean. And so they agreed verbally, even though they didn't communicate with each other because of a lack of the common language skill, that they would have a contract each in Korean and Vietnamese. And they each then signed the contract. The one provider who signed the contract was, let's say, the owner who was going to pay to have their house remodeled, and they have a misunderstanding. And the contractor who adheres to the Korean language says: I have a disagreement; you've not upheld your end of this contract. And the owner, who might have this contract that he understands in Vietnamese, says: You have not held up your end of the contract.

We remain the only country in the world that doesn't have an official language.

How do we litigate something like that within the courts of the United States of America when there is a disagreement on the interpretation between two languages that are not common languages in the United States but official languages of the countries where they came from?

Can we be litigating those kind of disagreements? Or can we simply say, a contract with the Federal Government is an official document; it shall be in English. If you choose to interpret that into another language for the purposes of the utility of your needs, that is fine with us, but we aren't going to litigate the difference in the courts of America because of people who refuse to use the official language of the United States, which needs to be established as English. . . .

Language and Culture

Here in this country, we remain the only country in the world that doesn't have an official language. We say English is our common language, but we have forces out here seeking to subdivide us, and we have billions of dollars that flow out of this Congress that go into the hands of people who are promoting division in America and not unity in America. The message that many immigrants get when they arrive here in this country is, if you learn English, and this message is clearly given as part of the debate here on the floor [of Congress], if you learn English, you give up your own culture. That is the message that we hear.

A common language binds us together.

Not true. In my neighborhood, I look around my neighborhood and certain communities that were ethnic enclaves when they were settled, German, Danish, Irish, Swedish, to name a few in my neighborhood, but the people that came here speaking a foreign language have adapted into English, and hardly any of them speak another language other than English that live there. But you could not convince them that they have given up their culture. You can't convince a German that their culture has changed dramatically because they have adhered to a common language here.

Now, I think utilization of other languages and language skills are a good thing, and I encourage young people to study foreign languages. I use that in the analysis of culture and use that in trade and use that in foreign travel and use that to help open up our negotiations and discussions and reduce the friction and the conflict from nation to nation. Those are all good things. But a common language within a country binds it together, and accepting English as our official language means that the people who do so are tied more to a common sense of history, more to a common cause. . . .

A common language binds us together. It lets us communicate for a common cause. It's going to move this Nation forward and make us more successful than we have been in the past. It preserves our culture, our history, our heritage. It gives us a common experience. It ties us to our history, and it lets an American go from corner to corner, from Maine to California and from Washington to Florida, and pick up a newspaper or walk into a store or a church or a park or a school or anywhere and be able to communicate in a common form of communications currency, at least with government. And if government uses the common form, the incentive will be there for others to use that common form.

2

The United States Should Not Have a National Language

Chris Donnelly

Chris Donnelly is a writer based in Connecticut.

Although many towns across the country are trying to, or already have made, English the official language, these English-only laws clearly violate Constitutional Amendments. In particular, Latino immigrants are targeted by these laws, which often lead to stigma and alienation. In some cases, English-only laws render those not proficient in English unemployable. In fact, many government officials do not realize that by enacting English-only laws they are harming businesses that rely on immigrant labor. The United States was established with a diverse population that should be celebrated, and a national language would not celebrate this diversity.

Just this past week [February 2007], Nashville, Tenn., and the quaint town of Pahrump, Nev., have been added to the roster of municipalities that tried to make English their official language. While many people just do not care about what happens in Pahrump or Nashville while living in Storrs, Conn., these and all previous cases are far more important to everyday life than any of us can imagine. The simple fact is, there is no official language in the United States, and there never should be one.

Many conservatives have argued that the influx of Hispanic immigrants is threatening our core American values, and that thus Americans must protect the sacred institution of the English language. The great Republican Senator of Tennessee, Lamar Alexander, was quoted in the *New York Times* as saying, "We're free to say what we want, speak what we want, but it is our national language." Apparently Alexander missed the high school civics class where the Constitution was read, for it says nowhere in it that English is the "national language." In fact, the Constitution states the contrary. According to the Fourteenth Amendment, "No state shall make or enforce any law which shall abridge the privileges of citizens of the United States." This amendment was created in the post-Civil War era to guarantee African-Americans the basic rights all U.S. citizens enjoy. This includes the Bill of Rights and the First Amendment, both of which protect freedom of expression. If people cannot freely express how they feel, then their Constitutional rights are clearly being violated. By making a national language, Congress would effectively be violating multiple Constitutional Amendments.

National Language and the Freedom of Speech

The fact that people are getting so hyped up about this is ridiculous, especially when in the past there have been many more controversial legal cases revolving around the freedom of speech. Take for example the case of *R.A.V. v. City of St. Paul, Minnesota*. In this case, the pride of St. Paul, 17-year-old Robert A. Viktora, decided to spend his free time exercising symbolic speech by burning a cross on the front lawn of an African American family's home. Besides the fact that he was a racist imbecile—he lived across the street from the people, not the least bit conspicuous—Viktora got off with a clean slate thanks to ever-progressive Supreme Court Justice Antonin Scalia. Scalia struck down a St. Paul statute equivalent to "fighting words," an exception to the protections of the First Amendment. Was there a massive congressional outrage to this decision? No. Is there a schism across the American landscape over saying "hola"? Yes. Besides the obvious racial implications—you do not see an upheaval over people speaking French or Creole on Bourbon Street—many Congressmen do not realize how a measure such as making English the national language would hurt them, and in particular their business interests.

> *The legislative effort to make English the official language is targeted largely at Latino immigrants who have not mastered the English language.*

As a once-Texan, I can assure you that Mexican and other Latino immigrants commonly get the worst jobs that our society has to offer, especially in the border states where many decide to settle. By building many of our houses, and doing much of our agricultural work, these immigrants are commonly paid as little as possible. Their language barrier is commonly used against them. By making English the official language, rich congressmen would be effectively making it extremely hard for poor Mexican and Latino immigrants to be exploited. In fact, they would be making it illegal to have any non-English speaking immigrants working for them in the first place.

Spanish-Speaking Immigrants Are Unfairly Targeted

For example, according to Occupational Safety and Health Standards for Shipyard Employment standard number 1915.16, there has to be an "[e]mployee comprehension of signs and labels. The Employer shall ensure that each sign or label posted to comply with the requirements of this subpart is presented in a manner that can be perceived and understood by all employees." By making the national language English, there would be no feasible way that Spanish speaking immigrants could ever understand exclusively English signs, therefore violating a federal statute. With English as the national language, Congress would create the potential of crippling the shipping and other crucial industries which employ non-English speaking workers—the very industries in which members of the legislature have vested interests.

An action would make immigrants less likely to come to America and work, and also make the lives of non-English speakers already here much harder. While many would hail this as a great thing, a crucial landmark in the protection of American essence, all that will happen is large corporations would suddenly lose a cheap workforce, and would have to start paying people appropriate wages. Many believe that the era of civil rights is over. Many Americans believe we have full equality. We do not. The legislative effort to make English the official language is targeted largely at Latino immigrants who have not mastered the English language. By separating them from the rest of the American population, it is making these people objects for ridicule and harassment. This is effectively segregation all over again.

By creating a national language, people from all over the world are now told "you are not welcome here."

All people are more or less the same. We all have dreams and aspirations, and we have all traveled here in an attempt to give us a better life.

By creating a national language, people from all over the world are now told "you are not welcome here." We will no longer be able to say, "Give me your tired, your poor, your huddled masses yearning to breathe free"—these words, inscribed upon the Statue of Liberty, will no longer have meaning.

The true essence of America is that we are a melting pot, and we should celebrate this diversity at every turn. We are

America because we are different. We are America because we do not have a national language.

3

Election Ballots Must Be Multilingual

Glenn D. Magpantay

Glenn D. Magpantay is a staff attorney with the Asian American Legal Defense and Education Fund, where he directs programs related to census and voting rights.

The population of Asian Americans is growing rapidly in the United States. Although many new citizens were enthusiastic about exercising their right to vote in the 2008 election, they faced several challenges on Election Day. Despite being required to assist voters with limited English proficiency by providing translated ballots and allowing translators in the booths, many counties failed to do so. All counties must comply with the Language Assistance Provisions as defined in the Voting Rights Act to ensure every American has the ability to vote during elections. Poll worker education, multilingual staff and proper materials are essential to ensuring that everyone has an opportunity to cast a vote.

Asian Americans are the fastest growing minority group in the United States. For almost two decades, AALDEF [Asian American Legal Defense and Education Fund] has monitored elections. We monitored for compliance with the language assistance provisions (section 203) of the federal Voting Rights Act, more recently for compliance with the Help America Vote Act (HAVA), and to document other incidents of anti-Asian voter disenfranchisement.

Glenn D. Magpantay, Hearing on "Lessons Learned from the 2008 Election," U.S. House of Representatives, Committee on the Judiciary, Subcommittee on the Constitution, Civil Rights, and Civil Liberties, March 19, 2009.

On November 4, 2008, AALDEF monitored over 229 poll sites and conducted a nonpartisan multilingual exit poll of 16,665 Asian American voters in 52 cities in 11 states—New York, New Jersey, Massachusetts, Pennsylvania, Michigan, Illinois, Texas, Nevada, Louisiana, Virginia, Maryland—and the District of Columbia. AALDEF received more than 800 complaints of voting barriers.

Specific efforts are needed to help Asian Americans fully participate in the electoral franchise.

Asian Americans are becoming U.S. citizens through naturalization and are registering to vote. According to the Census, Asian citizens of voting age numbered 3.9 million in 1996 and rose from 4.7 million in 2000 to 6.7 million in 2004. Asian American voter turnout also steadily increased, from 1.7 million in 1996, nearly 3 million in 2004, and 3.2 million in 2006. In AALDEF's 2008 exit poll, we found that almost a third (31%) of Asian American respondents were first-time voters.

We also found that 79% were foreign-born naturalized citizens and 21% had no formal U.S. education. Because of this, many Asian Americans were unfamiliar with the American electoral process, having come from Asian countries with political systems very different from that of the United States and which may even lack a tradition of voting. Some did not understand even basic political procedures, such as the need to register by a certain date, the need to enroll in a political party in order to vote in a primary election, and how to operate voting machines. Moreover, among voters surveyed, only 20% identified English as their native language; 35% were limited English proficient. Specific efforts are needed to help Asian Americans fully participate in the electoral franchise.

The Right to Language Assistance in the Voting Booth

In 1975, Congress enacted the language assistance provisions of the Voting Rights Act, codified at Section 203. In 2007, after extensive fact-finding into the continued disenfranchisement of Asian American and other minority voters, Congress reauthorized the Act for twenty-five more years. AALDEF provided evidence to Congress about the need for an extension of Section 203 to remove barriers to voting for Asian Americans.

Section 203 covers counties that have, according to the Census, 5% or more than 10,000 voting-age citizens who speak the same language, are limited English proficient, and, as a group, have a higher illiteracy rate than the national illiteracy rate as measured by educational attainment. Covered counties must translate ballots and all voting materials, including voter registration forms, instructions, and notices, into the covered language(s), as well as provide interpreters at poll sites to assist voters. Currently, five Asian language groups—Chinese, Japanese, Korean, Filipino, and Vietnamese—are covered in 16 counties in 7 states.

Section 203 has opened the political process to hundreds of thousands of Asian American voters, many of them new citizens. Partly due to Section 203's mandate for translated voter registration forms, Asian American voter registration growth from 1996 to 2004 was nearly 60%. This number led all other demographic groups (Hispanics at 44.6%, Blacks at 14.6%, and whites at 6.9%). Asian Americans also led in voter turnout growth at 71.2%, (Hispanics at 57.1%, Blacks at 25.6%, and whites at 15.0%).

According to AALDEF's 2008 exit poll, nearly one in five voters (18%) preferred voting with some form of language assistance in order to exercise their right to vote. The rates were higher in jurisdictions required to provide translated ballots.

Translated ballots have enabled Asian American voters to exercise their right to vote independently and privately inside the voting booth.

Voting Barriers on Election Day 2008

Notwithstanding such increased participation in the elections, Asian American voters continued to encounter several voting barriers in November 2008 in regard to language assistance, racist and poorly trained poll workers, inaccurate voter registration lists and denials of provisional ballots, improper and excessive identification checks, and confusion at poll sites.

Language assistance, such as interpreters or translated voting materials, if any, was far from adequate. Some poll workers were completely unaware of their legal responsibilities or outright refused to make language assistance available to voters.

New York and Boston are required to provide language assistance, but there were many shortcomings. New York is covered under Section 203 for assistance in Chinese and Korean. Boston is obligated to provide assistance in Chinese and Vietnamese pursuant to a settlement to remedy violations of Section 2 of the Voting Rights Act.

- At a poll site in the Lower East Side [New York City], there was only one interpreter for hundreds of voters. Poll workers tried to get additional interpreters but were told they "didn't need" them. The lone Chinese interpreter was extremely overworked. At another site in Jackson Heights, NY the poll site coordinator did not even know that a Korean interpreter was available at the site.

- Some interpreters did not effectively assist voters. In Houston, TX, two Vietnamese American voters stated that they were unable to vote for president even after requesting poll worker assistance.

- Poll workers in Dorchester, MA could not locate Vietnamese-language provisional ballots. They said these were not provided to them.

- In Boston, ballots did not have transliterations of candidates' names in Chinese. Limited English proficient voters typically know the candidates by their transliterated names, which often appear in Asian-language media. In our survey, ninety-five (95) Chinese voters stated that they had difficulty identifying their candidates of choice because the names were not transliterated. One voter in Chinatown remarked that new citizens were happy to have just been sworn in and were excited about voting but were disappointed to find that ballots were not fully translated.

More Voting Day Obstructions

Voters have the right to be assisted by persons of their choice under Section 208 of the Voting Rights Act. Unlike Section 203, this provision applies across the nation. These assistors may accompany voters inside the voting booth to translate the ballot for them. The only exception under this federal law is that they may not be the voters' union representatives or employers. Poll workers, however, obstructed this right.

- At one site in Alexandria, VA, poll workers did not allow limited English proficient voters to bring interpreters with them into the voting booth. Poll workers stated that individuals should have a minimum proficiency in English in order to be American citizens and to vote.

Many jurisdictions voluntarily provided language assistance to Asian American voters on November 4, 2008. For example:

- Chicago, IL hired election judges who spoke Gujarati, Hindi, Tagalog, Korean, Urdu, and Vietnamese.

- New Orleans, LA had about half a dozen Vietnamese interpreters and bilingual election commissioners.

- Lowell, MA hired about 20 Khmer and Vietnamese interpreters.

- Quincy, MA hired 15 Chinese and Vietnamese speaking poll workers.

- Middlesex, NJ appointed Chinese and Hindi/Gujarati speaking poll workers.

- Philadelphia, PA provided 30 Chinese, Khmer, Korean, and Vietnamese interpreters.

While we commend these efforts, there were also many shortcomings.

The lack of language assistance created opportunities to take advantage of limited English proficient voters for partisan gain.

- Bergen County [New Jersey] translates voting instructions into Korean. During the Presidential Primary Elections, one poll worker in Fort Lee, NJ did not even know why she received the Korean voting instructions.

- Under New Jersey state law, Voter Bill of Rights signs must be available and translated into the language spoken by 10% or more of registered voters in a district.

However, none of the 25 poll sites inspected in Bergen County provided a translated Voter Bill of Rights, even though translated signs were required by law.

- During the Presidential Primary Elections, Philadelphia provided a language line that poll workers could call and get on-the-spot assistance for voters. However, poll workers did not know it existed, did not know how to access the line, or the line was overwhelmed and was constantly busy. Voters in Olney [a neighborhood in North Philadelphia] left because they could not understand the ballots and were not able to get help.

- The lack of language assistance created opportunities to take advantage of limited English proficient voters for partisan gain. In Annandale, VA, limited English proficient Korean American senior citizens had to turn to a Republican campaigner for assistance. This person led groups of voters into the poll site and refused to give them privacy while they cast their votes. AALDEF received and reported similar complaints of improper voter influence during the 2006 elections by the same individual involved. . . .

Recommendations to Ensure Voter Rights

Several steps must be taken to address the barriers faced by Asian American voters. AALDEF makes the following recommendations.

1. National Recommendations

- The United States Supreme Court should uphold Section 5 of the Voting Rights Act [which requires federal review of voting changes]. Congress reauthorized the enforcement provision for 25 years in 2007 finding that racial, ethnic, and language minority voters continued to face voting discrimination and that the provision was necessary to protect the right to vote.

The provision is being challenged in *Northwest Austin Municipal Utility District One v. Holder*.

- Congress should consider legislation to allow for universal voter registration which will alleviate many of the registration problems that Asian American voters encountered.

- Congress should amend HAVA to clarify that voting by provisional ballot should also be used to correct errors and omissions in voters' registrations, as was recommended by the Carter/Ford National Commission on Federal Election Reform.

- The U.S. Department of Justice should continue its vigorous enforcement of Section 203 of the Voting Rights Act for Asian language assistance and increase enforcement of Section 208 to ensure that voters can be assisted by persons of their choice.

- The U.S. Department of Justice should more forcefully investigate and enforce full compliance with HAVA, including the proper and nondiscriminatory application of identification requirements and the availability of provisional ballots.

- The U.S. Election Assistance Commission should translate the national voter registration form into the federally required Asian languages.

2. Local Recommendations

- Language assistance should be provided to limited English proficient voters at the local level. There should be translated voter registration forms, voting instructions, and ballots, as well as interpreters and bilingual poll workers at poll sites.

- Poll workers who are rude, hostile, or racially discriminatory toward Asian American and limited English proficient voters, or who deny language assistance, should be reprimanded or removed from their posts.

• Voters whose names cannot be found in lists of registered voters located at poll sites must be given provisional ballots. Local election officials should count the ballots of all these registered voters when their ballots are cast in their neighborhoods and local districts, even if they were at the wrong poll sites.

• Errors in the registrations of new voters must be corrected so that ballots are not disqualified. Voting by provisional ballot should be used as opportunities to correct such errors.

• Poll workers need better training in election procedures and voters' rights, especially on:

• the requirements for language assistance and the proper use and posting of translated voting materials and signs under Section 203, where applicable;

• voters' rights to be assisted by persons of their choice, who may also accompany voters inside voting booths under Section 208;

• how to properly direct voters to their assigned poll sites and precinct voting booths;

• proper demands for voter identification checks under HAVA; and

• proper administration of provisional ballots under HAVA.

Asian American populations have surged throughout the United States. Asian Americans are becoming citizens and seek to participate in the nation's political franchise, but they have encountered many voting barriers. The findings and recommendations herein will hopefully assist the [U.S. House of Representatives] Committee [on the Judiciary] in ensuring that Asian Americans, and indeed all Americans, can fully and fairly exercise their right to vote.

4

Multilingualism Is Bad for the United States

Franklin Raff

Franklin Raff is a senior producer for Radio America and the executive producer of the G. Gordon Liddy Show.

Through advertising and political campaigns, Americans are being made to believe that immigrants are learning English while preserving their languages of origin. However, this is far from true in most cases. Many Hispanics in particular are not learning English, which causes comprehension problems in emergency rooms as well as many on-the-job accidents—sometimes with fatal results. Families who do not immediately immerse their children in English are doing them a disservice because these children tend to do poorly both in school and later in the job market. A multilingual nation does not benefit individuals or America as a whole.

On Super Bowl Sunday [February 5, 2006], Toyota debuts what it calls the nation's first "bi-cultural, bilingual" advertisement.

The spot shows a father talking to his son, in English and Spanish, about the benefits of the new car:

"Papa, Why do we have a hybrid?"

"For your future . . . It's better for the air, and, we spend less because it runs on gas and electrical power. It uses both."

"Like you, with English and Spanish!"

Franklin Raff, "American 'Multilingualism': A National Tragedy," WorldNetDaily, February 5, 2006. Copyright © 2006 WorldNetDaily.com, Inc. Reproduced by permission.

"Si!"

Toyota vice president Jim Farley says the spot "incorporates the truth that parents are always moving forward in their lives, and we think the commercial will really resonate across cultural lines and show the benefits of our new Camry Hybrid in a touching and effective way."

Sadly, with every legal and cultural step we take to make life more immediately convenient for non-English speaking immigrants, we merely feed the beast.

Bilingual Issues

Toyota's ad agency may realize it's on shaky ground: Papa ultimately tells his son he learned English, too, for the child's future. This end note is nearly laudable, but it does not make the "big idea" of the spot any less misleading. Parents aren't always moving forward in their lives—especially parents that do not have the discipline to allow their children to be immersed, completely and immediately, in the English language. The fruits of our "touching" national love affair with bilingualism are not limited to voice-mail purgatories, non-English speaking local government offices, and billions of tax dollars literally lost "in translation". Some effects are in fact, deadly: A recent study by the journal *Pediatrics* indicates that translation errors between doctors, parents, and patients are common and often dangerous, even when translators are involved. Emergency rooms across the country are plagued by the triage nightmare of "spanglish" (the word intoxicado, for instance, means "poisoned," not "intoxicated"), and OSHA [Occupational Safety and Health Administration] reports yearly increases in the number of Hispanics and immigrants killed on the job, largely because of safety comprehension problems.

Sadly, with every legal and cultural step we take to make life more immediately convenient for non-English speaking immigrants, we merely feed the beast. Chicago's public school system, for instance, holds a mind-boggling fifty-seven thousand English as a Second Language children and consistently ranks "dead last" among the nation's forty-seven largest school districts. Their biggest concern right now? Filling more and more "bilingual special education" positions.

Bilingualism can be marvelous. I have warm memories of my bilingual youth in French-speaking Quebec [Canada]. I was immersed completely in 6th grade and, as kids will, I became "proficient" in the span of a few months. But let us not fool ourselves, and let's not allow Toyota to believe they're honing in on a qualified demographic. How common is the portrait of a Latino family cruising along in a new, $25,000 hybrid? According to a recent Federal Deposit Insurance Company study, although Hispanics comprise the country's largest minority group, almost half of them—or twenty million people—have not even opened a bank account.

So let me take you out of a hybridized, high-income fantasy world, for a moment, and paint a few "touching" and honest pictures of the state of "bilingualism" in our country. There's an office janitor in our building with whom I regularly exchange pleasantries. He speaks no English, but he understands my Italian and I understand his Spanish. He is poor, but he is a fast, meticulous, and good-natured worker. I had always imagined him as somewhat indentured, at first to a coyote [someone who specializes in smuggling immigrants across the border from Mexico into the United States], perhaps, and now, thanks to a language barrier, to his foreman. But—I learned recently—he has in fact been in this country since he was a baby. Impoverished, unable to scan the "want" ads, but perfectly able to converse with our local Spanish-speaking social services and food stamp officials, he continues to enjoy the fruits of American-style bilingualism.

Let me introduce you to the sweet little girl in my supermarket. She's standing right next to me, and she's too small to reach the upper shelf. When I ask her if I can help, she can only stare at me quizzically. She isn't deaf. She appears to be a normal third or fourth-grader. But she has been permanently disabled in the name of some vague sense of multicultural heterogeneity. I bet you have experienced a moment just like this. I want you to remember that feeling in your heart when you realize you are smiling, in a sense, at a ghost. I want to remind you, in this case, that the misunderstood word is "Help." How does it feel to know that our tax dollars, our media landscape, and our "feel good" cultural approach to bilingualism are destroying her future?

Multilingualism is crippling us, individually and collectively.

Language Immersion in the Schools

Despite a Pew/Kaiser poll indicating that 90 percent of Latinos feel they need to learn English to succeed in the United States, California is now touting a "dual immersion" program in which first-grade classes are taught ninety-percent in Spanish. That's right. Your kids are forced to learn Spanish, while their Spanish-speaking classmates, year by year, are gently weaned off the mother tongue. If, that is, they make it through school that far. In an age in which college education is a prerequisite to the middle class, Harvard's Civil Rights Project's latest report says that Hispanics are dropping out of school at an astonishing—and increasing—rate. Only half of the Latino kids entering ninth grade will actually graduate. And despite national increases in college matriculation, only about one in twelve Hispanics currently enrolled in public school—according to the folks at Harvard, at least—will go on to earn a college degree. One in twelve. How does that feel?

Marketers, ad agencies, and media outlets stretch the truth as a matter of course. It is not done with malevolence. I run a small ad agency. I know how easy it can be to get swept up in the joy of the creative process, and sometimes, in the pleasure of an envisioned reality. Nor do advertising executives—and "executive creatives," as we are known—generally live in neighborhoods where we see, on a daily basis, the living result of the lie of "bilingualism." But in this case, the lie is deadly. It's deadly because it leads us to believe that, despite the accidents and deaths, despite the lost opportunities, despite the skyrocketing expenditures, despite rampant poverty and heartbreak, despite all this, all is well in our "multilingual" nation. All is not well.

Multilingualism Is Bad for America

Multilingualism is crippling us, individually and collectively. It might feel good, temporarily, to think otherwise, just as it might feel good, temporarily, to think you are saving the earth by purchasing a type of vehicle which—according to *Consumer Reports*—will probably deliver nineteen miles less, on average, per gallon, under actual driving conditions, than its advertised EPA [U.S. Environmental Protection Agency] rating. You should buy whatever car you like. But don't let those snappy Madison Avenue creatives fool you into feeling good about bilingualism. It is not a cultural boon. It is a national tragedy.

5

The United States Benefits from Multilingual Americans

Rowena Alegria

Rowena Alegria is a third-generation Denver native and editor of the Spanish-language weekly Viva Colorado.

Although some critics view a multilingual American as a threat, most parents report wanting their child to learn a second language. The United States as a whole would do well to encourage immigrants to maintain their native languages as they learn English. Being multilingual benefits individuals who need to compete in the global marketplace, and having a multilingual population also would help protect national security, as was seen after the terrorist attacks on September 11, 2001.

If you speak English only, ordering a Big Mac and fries just isn't what it used to be. Nor is getting extra pillows at a hotel or calling customer service about the phone bill. Even the NFL [National Football League] is now airing commercials in Spanish—with English subtitles.

Suddenly, it seems, Spanish is everywhere. Along with those who speak it.

What does that mean for the English language in the United States, where 251 million people, or about 96 percent of the population, speak English?

Probably nothing.

Rowena Alegria, "It's a Multilingual World, After All," *Denver Post*, September 30, 2007. Reproduced by permission of the author.

The Loss of Native Languages

Spanish, like German and Italian and every other language that has been absorbed by the melting pot that is this country, is not a threat to English in America. Today's immigrants are the parents and grandparents of tomorrow's proud Americans, who study after study have shown will speak English. And English only.

Since 1990, the Hispanic population of the United States has doubled, to 42.7 million (counting historical and immigrant populations). Growth in the Southwest—Colorado included—has been notable. The U.S. Census says Anglos are now a minority in Denver. The city's public school system, with a Hispanic enrollment of 57.3 percent, reflects that.

But immigration comes in waves. And this is by no means the first wave.

Immigrants come to the United States because they want to live the American dream. Even if they have illusions of maintaining their ways, they and their children soon learn that their native culture and language are considered inferior here. To succeed and be accepted as American, they must learn English.

And when it comes to language, "The assimilative power of American society is overwhelming," wrote Ruben G. Rumbaut and Alejandro Portales, professors of sociology at the University of California-Irvine, and Princeton, respectively.

Rumbaut and Portales were referring in particular to results from the Children of Immigrants Longitudinal Study of 2006, a decade-long project that examined in-depth the interaction between immigrant parents and children and the evolution of the young from adolescence into early adulthood in San Diego and Miami. The study found that fully two-thirds—64.8 percent—of second-generation young people indicated that they prefer to speak English only.

The finding corroborated multiple studies of immigrants and language, including 2000 Census data on Mexican-

Americans, all showing that the mother tongue is extinguished in favor of English by the third generation—even in Los Angeles, the largest Spanish-speaking enclave in the United States.

The benefits of speaking English in this country just cannot be overstated or denied. Despite efforts by some commercial, governmental and educational entities to accommodate Spanish speakers, most of this country's business is conducted in English, and if you cannot participate you are at a tremendous disadvantage. Lost in translation is not a place you want to be if your child has been in an accident and you need to communicate with the police, the insurance company, and doctors and nurses.

The Benefits of Remaining Multilingual

Nonetheless, our nation's propensity to be a "graveyard" for language may come to haunt us in the 21st century, as technology all but erases the historical hurdle of distance across the globe and pits our best and brightest against those from everywhere else in the world.

Immediately following Sept. 11, [2001, when terrorists attacked the United States] for example, we found ourselves completely unprepared linguistically to respond to the attack. The CIA [Central Intelligence Agency], FBI [Federal Bureau of Investigation] and NSA [National Security Agency] could not even talk with, let alone penetrate, "terrorist cells" because they lacked employees who could speak the necessary languages.

In December 2006, an Iraq Study Group report noted that, "all of our efforts in Iraq, military and civilian, are handicapped by Americans' lack of knowledge of language and cultural understanding . . . in a conflict that demands effective and efficient communication." The report recommended that the federal government make professional language proficiency a high priority.

---

75 percent of American adults want their own children to become fluent in a second language before graduating from high school.

The economic reality also cannot be ignored. A report commissioned by the British Council last year said monolingual English graduates "face a bleak economic future" as multilingual competitors flood the world's marketplaces. The report, titled "English Next," cited the massive increase in the number of people learning English worldwide. More than half of all Chinese primary school students learn English, for example.

"The competitive advantage of speaking English is ebbing away," said linguistic consultant and report author David Graddol. "Once everyone speaks English, advantage can only be maintained by having something else—other skills, such as speaking several languages."

Apparently, many Americans already understand the value of knowing more than one language. In fact, 75 percent of American adults want their own children to become fluent in a second language before graduating from high school, according to a 2000 General Social Survey cited in a report to Congress earlier this year. Sixty-four percent of those surveyed believe that learning a foreign language is as valuable as math and science in school. And 78 percent strongly disagree that public school bilingual-education programs should be eliminated.

More than two out of three disagree with the following: "English is threatened if other languages are used frequently in large immigrant communities in the U.S." Seventy-six percent also believe that "speaking English as the common national language is what unites all Americans."

Perhaps it is time to move past the rhetoric and realize that if we have anything to fear at all it is that the English-only movement might hamper our prospects for peace and prosperity in the next millennium.

6

Addressing Multilingualism in Religious Communities Is Challenging

Annie Gowen

Annie Gowen is a writer for the Washington Post.

Holding a church service that meets the needs of people from different backgrounds and the needs of people who speak different languages is challenging. It's both challenging for those planning the service as well as for those attending. However, it is worth the effort. Building a small multiethnic and multilingual community such as a church can bring together people who might not otherwise have talked with one another—thus bringing the whole community outside the church doors closer together.

When Calvary Baptist Church first tried to integrate its Sunday morning services for English and Spanish speakers, the result was misery for all. The congregants grew restless as they sat through endless translation from one language to the other. The service dragged on for 90 minutes. Nobody knew the hymns.

Complaints raged.

"I don't understand what they're saying on the pulpit." "I don't know the words of the hymns." "Why are we singing in

Spanish?" longtime parishioners of the historic church in downtown Washington [D.C.] told pastor Amy Butler.

Nonetheless, Butler was determined to persevere, gambling her seven years of progress rebuilding the fading congregation into a 200-member mix of urban hipsters, Latino families and tradition-loving seniors. Would the move to full-time bilingual services further fuel Calvary's growth, or prompt an exodus of disgruntled worshipers?

Calvary is at the vanguard of a nascent but growing movement toward multiculturalism in American worship that some believe is the wave of the future.

"Every time we face a challenge such as this, I stay up at night worrying about it," said Butler, 40, who made the switch permanent in January [2010]. "We felt this multiracial, multiethnic expression of our faith was true to what God has called us to do in this place. It's very important that what's being reflected inside our sanctuary is similar to what's going on on the outside."

In choosing to integrate its Spanish speakers into the main congregation rather than holding separate services, Calvary is at the vanguard of a nascent but growing movement toward multiculturalism in American worship that some believe is the wave of the future.

Churches and Segregation

But other theologians and experts say there are profound cultural reasons why—as the Rev. Martin Luther King Jr. famously observed—11 a.m. on Sunday remains "the most segregated hour" in the nation. Even as waves of immigrants from Latin America, Asia and Africa have made the country vastly more diverse, fewer than 10 percent of churches reflect those demographic changes, experts believe.

"Churches are still overwhelmingly segregated," said Korie Edwards, a professor of sociology at Ohio State University and the author of *The Elusive Dream: The Power of Race in Interracial Churches*. "They may say that they're committed to racial and ethnic diversity, but making that a reality is a different story."

Michael Emerson, a sociology professor at Rice University, conducted a national survey in 2007 and found that just 7 percent of congregations consider themselves multiracial, and that churches are likely to have a mere fraction of the diversity of the neighborhoods surrounding them. Over the years, he has seen congregations torn apart by efforts to integrate, especially when it involves language.

"People have to worship via the vehicle of culture. When you start mixing culture, language and worship style, people feel their culture is not being represented, and they're less comfortable with it, even when you're trying to balance it," he said. "It's hard to sustain."

Proponents of multicultural services say that churches—especially those in urban neighborhoods like Calvary's—must diversify to survive as the country grows less homogeneous. But what form that integration will take is a matter of hot debate.

Traditionally, churches wanting to reach out to minority groups have held separate foreign language services. The Archdiocese of Washington [D.C.], for example, has Mass in 20 languages, but bilingual services are rare.

"Generally, everybody wants to go to Mass in their own language if they can do it," said Monsignor Mark Brennan, pastor of St. Martin of Tours Catholic Church in Gaithersburg [Md.]. About four times a year, the church has a special multilingual service in English, Spanish and French, which is "wonderful," Brennan said, but a logistical nightmare.

He has sometimes found himself standing at the altar not sure what language the choir would sing in next.

The Growth of Multilingual Services

Blending cultures and languages in worship is "still ahead of the mainstream, but there's growing interest and growing intent," said Mark DeYmaz, author of the book *Ethnic Blends: Mixing Diversity into Your Local Church.*

His church, housed in a former Kmart in Little Rock [Ark.], displays the flags of more than 30 countries at its services, which feature readings translated into Spanish and sign language, a Chinese teaching pastor and a gospel choir.

DeYmaz said he's aware some might find this melting pot worship style distracting or off-putting. "While it's certainly easier to go to church with people who are just like you," he said, "pursuing what's right from a Christian perspective has never been about what's easy."

On a recent spring Sunday morning at Calvary Baptist, Latino and Burmese families bowed their heads next to single professionals from the bustling gentrified neighborhood around Verizon Center, where the red-spired church sits on the corner of Eighth and H streets. Sprinkled among them were older, mostly white members in dresses and suits who had been coming there for decades.

They gamely recited Spanish prayer responses printed in the program and sang, "Make us one, Lord, make us one."

So far, Butler said, she doesn't know of anyone who has left Calvary because of the bilingual blending, despite the complaints. But the church has trimmed its service back to an hour and added a simultaneous translation in Spanish on little headphones to make it more palatable.

Even so, English speakers dive for their Bibles when readings are in Spanish to find the translation. And they sit there lost at times when associate pastor Edgar Palacios, from El Salvador, does the sermon in his native tongue.

Some members of the congregation said that the blended service has brought them closer, and they now socialize outside of church.

Claudia Moore, 59, a retired high school librarian from Springfield [Va.] and a Calvary member for 48 years, said that the new service "took some getting used to," though she didn't consider leaving.

"I'd have to be honest and say I was less enthusiastic about going to church," she said. "But I'm trying not to be a stick in the mud."

Some members of the congregation said that the blended service has brought them closer and they now socialize outside of church.

Difficulties with Multicultural Services

But few Latinos come to the church's small weekly prayer groups, scattered in homes around the city, or serve on its boards. Even something simple such as the Easter potluck menu, for which eggs and ham are traditional, can spark debate.

"The Spanish families wanted to know, 'What does 'brunch food' mean? Can we bring refried beans?'" Butler said. "At the end of the day we decided everyone should bring what they like to eat on Easter."

After a bilingual blessing that Butler said they are still trying to perfect, the congregation moved into the meeting hall next door for coffee and doughnuts.

Virginia Teller, 79, a District resident and retired teacher, said she had become closer with one of the Latino families in the congregation; they now go thrift-shopping together. But she hoped that the church would not add any more Spanish to the service.

We don't want to be separate. . . . We want to integrate with the greater community.

"I will take what they have now but *no more*," she said. "Enough is enough! It is America. I feel everyone should try and speak English."

Jose Nunez, 39, a construction worker from Hyattsville [Md.], said in Spanish he was coming to the church's bilingual service to do just that.

"We don't want to be separate," he said. "We want to integrate with the greater community." Calvary, he said, has an "open heart."

7

English-Speaking Americans Do Not Need to Learn a Foreign Language

Jay Nordlinger

Jay Nordlinger, a senior editor with the National Review, *writes about politics, foreign affairs, and the arts.*

Many Americans feel ashamed about being monolingual, especially because many Europeans can speak English regardless of their native language. Americans should not feel embarrassed, however, about speaking English only. Europeans are exposed to more languages naturally through their proximity to other countries, which both creates a need to be multilingual and also makes learning languages easier. Likewise, in the United States, many people living in border towns are bilingual. Also, English speakers do not need to learn a foreign language because English is spoken globally.

Barack Obama was engaged in one of his favorite pastimes: lecturing Americans on their inadequacies. He said, "Instead of worrying about whether immigrants can learn English—they'll learn English—you need to make sure your child can speak Spanish. You should be thinking about, how can your child become bilingual? We should have every child speaking more than one language." He went on, "It's embarrassing when Europeans come over here. They all speak English—they speak French, they speak German. And then we go over to Europe. And all we can say is, 'Merci beaucoup.'"

A quarter of Americans can speak a language other than English well enough to hold a conversation.

It's embarrassing, says [former] Senator Obama. There is a certain type of American who is always embarrassed, especially in front of Europeans. We've all seen them. "Oh, we're so fat, we're so loud, we're so unsophisticated. We use ketchup, we don't know what to do with a bidet, we have the death penalty!" And "we don't learn foreign languages!" Most of these Americans are young and callow, and grow out of these attitudes. But many do not—and Mr. and Mrs. Obama seem like unreformed college students, in so many ways.

This issue of foreign languages is one of many clubs with which to beat Americans. According to the Gallup organization, a quarter of Americans can speak a language other than English well enough to hold a conversation. That doesn't seem so bad to me, all things considered. But be that as it may.

The Push to Learn a Foreign Language

Americans have long been jittery about their relationship with foreign languages. It is part of their self-examination, which, in a sickly form, is an inferiority complex. Earlier this decade, the U.S. Senate was moved to declare a year (2005) the "Year of Foreign Language Study." There was a time, about 15 years before that, when people were saying that Americans would have to learn Japanese. That was when Michael Dukakis was running political ads with an ominous rising sun. And I remember a football game, shown on television one Saturday afternoon.

During halftime, each university got to brag about itself with a video. Notre Dame, I believe, showed one of its students—an ordinary white kid—speaking Japanese. He narrated the video, and the rest of us got subtitles.

Soon, Japan went kaput (sort of), and Americans focused their worries elsewhere.

Some of us study foreign languages for the same reason others collect butterflies or play tennis: It's fun. Moreover, there are practical benefits, such as being strengthened in your home language. I believe I have studied five languages, formally—and maybe the same number informally. I hope to do more. But I reject the idea that Americans are especially guilty on the foreign-language front. There are differences between us and the Europeans: For us, the study of foreign languages is mainly a matter of choice; for them, it is something else.

All the world's languages come to the United States— because all the world's people do.

Europeans Are Multilingual Out of Necessity

America is a great big continental nation, stretching from the Atlantic to the Pacific. On our northern border, there is another vast continental nation, and it's almost entirely English-speaking. On our southern border, there is a Spanish-speaking country, plus the Gulf of Mexico. And guess what? Along our (short) border with Quebec, there is a fair amount of bilingualism—English and French. Along our (longer) border with Mexico, there's a fair amount of bilingualism—English and Spanish.

Exactly what you would expect. Because this is how these things work. If Europeans know foreign languages, it's not necessarily out of intellectual virtue; it's because the languages come naturally. A Swiss person—to take an easy example— lives in a small country with four official languages. A Nebraskan lives in a big state in the middle of a gigantic nation, and is a long, long way from other languages. But we should remember, too, that all the world's languages come to the United States—because all the world's people do.

The incentive to learn English is great, the incentive to learn other languages, not so great.

Back to Europe for a moment: Eric Hobsbawm, the celebrated hard-Left British historian, was once praised for knowing foreign languages. One of his sharpest critics, David Pryce-Jones, pointed out that "Hobsbawm has mastered only some of the main European languages, a feat shared by lots of restaurant waiters, never mind academics." Furthermore, sometimes language is imposed, against the will of the people. Many Eastern Europeans won't breathe a word of Russian, though they know it (and despite the fact that Russian is a great world language).

The Global Necessity of English

Consider this, too: For better or worse—and I say better—English is the world's lingua franca [common language]. And that bears on Americans and foreign languages. We are born into a language that virtually the entire world speaks or seeks to speak. For many, many of the world's people, it is a sine qua non [indispensable]. (Pardon my Latin.) The incentive to learn English is great, the incentive to learn other languages, not so great.

Incidentally, are you familiar with the old problem in Paris? You speak to them in French, and they answer you in English (however badly). You speak to them in English, and you'll get a stream of offended French from them. Sometimes, being an American means not being able to win.

I could tell 500 stories about the primacy of English in the world, but will tell you only this—my favorite. One afternoon, I was part of a small group of journalists who met with Alvaro Uribe, the president of Colombia. This was at the Annual Meeting of the World Economic Forum in Davos (Switzerland, as it happens). Before our session began, it became clear to me that I was the only non-Spanish speaker in the room. Not only that, I was the only non-native Spanish speaker in the room. I moved to leave. But Uribe insisted I stay—presidential order. And he, his cabinet members, the Latin American journalists, and I talked for an hour in English. No one batted an eye or so much as groped for a word. Amazing.

More Criticisms of Americans

By the way, another charge against Americans is that they don't know geography—that we don't know geography. A couple of months ago, Omar Sharif, the Egyptian-born actor, was on Arab television. Chances are, he didn't think any American could hear him—but, thanks to the Middle East Media Research Institute and its translations, we did. Sharif, who made a fortune off America, said,

> [America] is a large and rich country, with great possibilities and everything, but they don't understand what's going on in the rest of the world. They just don't get it. I lived in America for a long time. Only 10 percent of Americans have a passport. In other words, 90 percent have never left America. . . . You show them an unmarked map of Europe and ask them where France is, and they don't know. Ask them where Italy is—okay, Italy they know, because it looks like a shoe. They don't know anything. They are ignorant.

First, Italy looks more like a boot than a shoe. Second, the United States—those 50—is itself kind of a geography quiz. Third, would Sharif like to put the general geographical knowledge of the average Egyptian or Arab up against that of the average American? How about simple literacy?

Not long after hearing about this Sharif interview, I was with some Lebanese in Long Island, N.Y. One said he had heard that Americans knew nothing about geography, but found this wasn't true. Another said, "That's because you're in New York. If you were in the Midwest . . ."—and she said "Midwest" as though she was describing the farthest reaches of the Sahara. I remarked that I was from the Midwest, and so was my sister (her friend). She just smiled, weakly.

Incidentally, not 10 percent, but about a third of Americans hold a passport. And that reminds me of one of the most depressing encounters I ever had. It was with a young U.S. Foreign Service officer in a European country. He maintained that Republicans, in particular, were ignorant of the world, and liked it that way. He said that GOP [Republican] congressmen bragged about not having a passport. I said I doubted it.

At another point in the conversation, I mentioned a second Foreign Service officer, who was hoping to be posted back to the United States. The reason? His two sons, about ten and eight, had never lived in America, and he wanted them to know their country. My guy—the Republicans-and-passports guy—snorted, "Yeah—introduce 'em to the joys of Burger King." I said, "Do you really think that's all there is to American culture?" He said, "Well, there's jazz." "Anything else?" I asked. He said he couldn't think of anything.

He then said that all American children should be required to live abroad—all of them. I said, "How about the children of other countries? Should they, too, be required to live abroad?" He looked annoyed.

Americans Need to Be More Self-Confident

We are all familiar with the self-hating American (although, in my experience, these people aren't really self-hating, but rather supremely self-loving—they are just embarrassed to be American). But it is depressing indeed when they represent the U.S. abroad. Stupid college kids may put a Canadian maple leaf on their backpack, but American diplomats should be more mature. What's more, I believe that Americans who denigrate their country are less respected by foreigners than they think they are.

8

Bilingual Education Does Not Help Students

Greg Collins

Greg Collins is a 2009 graduate of the University of Massachu-setts–Amherst where he contributed to the Massachusetts Daily Collegian *and served as the president of the Republican Club.*

Bilingual education is receiving renewed focus because immigra-tion reform is again one of the top political topics currently be-fore our elected officials. Although bilingual education attempts to help those students not yet proficient in English, in reality it prevents students from successfully learning English at all. While this in no way means that people should not learn and maintain their native languages, it should not be done at the expense of learning English. Becoming fluent in English is essential for bet-ter paying jobs and financial independence. Immigrants are ca-pable of learning English, and to suggest otherwise is an insult.

If any one policy trivializes and patronizes immigrants, it is bilingual education. Possible presidential hopeful Newt Gin-grich re-ignited this issue recently when he spoke to the Na-tional Federation of Republican Women in Washington [D.C.] last week [March 31, 2007] saying, "The American people be-lieve English should be the official language of the govern-ment ... We should replace bilingual education with immer-sion in English so people learn the common language of the country and they learn the language of prosperity, not the language of living in a ghetto."

As immigration reform has risen to be one of the leading and most contentious political topics confronting current politicians and presidential candidates, bilingual education deserves to be re-examined. Continuing to enforce this policy is counterproductive towards encouraging assimilation among immigrants, which hurts both themselves and the future of the United States.

Mastering English enables immigrants to acquire the necessary skills to work at higher-skilled jobs to improve their socioeconomic status and to become financially independent.

Where Bilingual Education Fails

The goal of bilingual education programs that teach students mathematics and reading in their native language, like Spanish, is to ensure they do not fall behind their classmates in these subjects. But attempting to keep pace with their classmates in this regard stunts their growth in learning the most important subject of all, which is of course English.

We are all aware of the benefits of becoming proficient in English, as it strengthens communication among all Americans and provides a deep bond to convey our feelings in a mutually comprehensible fashion. Taking into account tangible, real world benefits, mastering English enables immigrants to acquire the necessary skills to work at higher-skilled jobs to improve their socioeconomic status and to become financially independent. Immigrants will be able to start families and provide for them without depending on government programs.

But bilingual education supporters gloss over these facts by sacrificing long term ramifications for short term benefits. In the short run students will not face the difficulties and high expectations of mastering English. But when these people encounter situations in which proficiency in English is a necessary prerequisite to fulfill the task at hand, whether it is writing an essay in college or responding to a customer's request at a restaurant, they will be left behind by people who already know the language.

Bilingual education supporters claim that they want to ease the transition of immigrants from their homeland to America. However, enforcing programs that de-emphasize the significance of a skill proven to be a crucial factor in earning high grades or getting hired does more to inhibit this transition than bilingual educators would care to admit.

One must be reminded that enforcing mastery in English does not devalue or denigrate the language and customs of the immigrants' past.

Policies Prevent Immigrants from Learning English

We shouldn't lambaste employees or students who do not speak English very well when educators and politicians enact policies to reflect a concern for feeling good about other people rather than having a genuine concern for helping immigrants transition to America in the quickest possible fashion. It is entirely logical why immigrants would not absorb the English language as quickly as they would normally when politicians and School Board members discourage assimilation into American society. Why would individuals feel the need to learn English quickly when programs are designed specifically to inhibit this growth? Progressives claim their policies reflect the needs and wishes of immigrants and the poor, but it is programs like bilingual education that explicitly promote laziness and irresponsibility for failing to adapt to a new culture.

One must be reminded that enforcing mastery in English does not devalue or denigrate the language and customs of the immigrants' past. There are many language programs in the U.S. available for people who want to learn their native language.

But feeling neutral about whether or not to enforce proficiency in English undermines the roots which have provided the foundation for the rise and maintenance of America as the most unified nation in the world. Our Founding Fathers and the Puritans who formed the original communities of this country would have found it reprehensible if they were told that this nation's educators were subsidizing education primarily taught in Spanish or any language besides English.

Instead, mandating education taught exclusively in English affirms the uniqueness of a country that enables people of all different backgrounds to not only embrace the most commonly spoken language in this country. It also allows legal immigrants to enter into an implicit but deeply powerful covenant with other Americans who will help their newly assimilated Americans in times of need. This would be the seminal milestone for an immigrant who was attracted to America because of its freedoms and national unity.

Immigrants Are Capable of More

Bilingual education is a tacit way of saying that only a certain group of people have the capabilities of becoming completely immersed Americans, and that immigrants should not be held up to the same standards as American-born children who also face the expectation of learning English.

The issue is not whether immigrants will struggle to learn English, because most assuredly they will. However, countless immigrants, including many of our descendents, have admirably confronted and conquered this challenge. Through the adaptation of learning English, immigrants have embraced American conceptions of morality, virtue, and liberal democracies. To expect anything less from immigrants is insulting and patronizing to their souls.

9

Students Have a Right to Use Their Native Language

Christina M. Rodriguez

Christina M. Rodriguez is an associate professor of law at the New York University School of Law. Her works include The Significance of the Local in Immigration Regulation *and* E Pluribus Unum: How Bilingualism Strengthens American Democracy.

While schools are required to provide funding to support English-language learners, schools often are ill-equipped to provide quality services. Also, people have the right to preserve their culture though language, but language services are intended to support English learners only until they have a working knowledge of the language. Although the United States has long recognized the importance of teaching English to non-native speakers, the importance of preserving native languages often is overlooked.

Question: *How do language policies in education create inequities for participants of differing language minority communities?*

The public schools are required by law to ensure equal access to education for all linguistic minority students. In *Lau v. Nichols* in 1974, the Supreme Court found that the San Francisco schools had violated their obligations under Title VI of the Civil Rights Act of 1964 by failing to provide adequate

English language instruction for students of Chinese parentage. Since Lau, Department of Education regulations have obligated schools to fulfill the decision's promise, and today's No Child Left Behind Act requires local schools to provide language instruction that increases English language proficiency and overall academic achievement.

But despite an elaborate legal framework intended to guide the decision making of local school districts in pursuit of these equality goals, inequities inevitably arise, for two primary reasons. First, linguistic minorities who make up a small percentage of a local school district's population can be more difficult to serve directly. Not only is Federal funding contingent on the percentage of English language learners (ELLs) in the student population, resources in the form of qualified teachers are also less plentiful for students whose native languages are not widely spoken minority languages like Spanish or Mandarin. In school districts with deeply diverse student populations, moreover, smaller minorities are less likely to be served with programs tailored specifically to their needs and with teachers adept in that minority's language. That said, among the pathologies attributed to bilingual education is the isolation of linguistic minority students from the larger student population for years at a time—a fate more likely to affect students who come from a heavily represented minority group, namely Spanish speakers.

Second, and more important, because ELLs are more likely to attend poor performing or under-resourced schools, their educational development is more likely to suffer as the result of general inequities in the system. Language programs often disserve ELLs not because bilingual education is an inherently flawed method of instruction, but because of "inept, passive-aggressive, or outright hostile administration," tendencies compounded by lack of funding and overcrowding. This larger problem of educational inequity is made worse by the persistence of de facto segregated schools. And, in the case of language minorities in particular, uneven access to quality language instruction is exacerbated by the fact that immigrant children today, in unprecedented numbers, live in parts of the United States today with little to no experience educating ELLs. Indeed, the dramatic rise in the number of ELLs in the so-called new immigration states, such as Georgia and North Carolina, fuels state and local efforts to crack down on illegal immigration, in large part because the rising ELL population is taxing the public schools in unfamiliar ways.

Parents and local school officials should be free to elect the culture they pass on to their children.

Question: Most people want to participate in the institutions of civic life, so it is important to provide them with the opportunity to learn English. At the same time, what language rights does one have if she wants to maintain her own culture through language?

To the extent that a right to protect one's culture exists, it can be located in the principle of intimate, familial association recognized as part of the ordered liberty guaranteed by the Due Process Clause of the Fourteenth Amendment. In *Meyer v. Nebraska*, a foundational case protecting this liberty interest, the Supreme Court struck down a state law that prohibited the teaching of any modern language other than English before the ninth grade. The court recognized not only the liberty of the language teacher to engage in instruction, as well as the student's right to acquire knowledge, but also the parent's right to control his or her child's education. The court thus acknowledged that parents have a "profound interest in cultural transmission," and that parental autonomy has served as the vehicle through which cultural pluralism has persisted in the United States. In a sense, Meyer acknowledges that a language lives or dies in the educational sphere, and that parents and local school officials should be free to elect the culture they pass on to their children.

This negative liberty is limited as a means of preserving culture through language, however—a limitation evident when we compare the American approach to the language rights protected by the constitution of Canada. The Charter of Rights and Freedoms establishes that French and English have equal status throughout Canada, reflecting a constitutional commitment to the survival of both languages. Among the mechanisms for preserving the minority French language is the constitutional guarantee of the right to an education in one's mother tongue, whether French or English, and the corresponding right to minority-run schools. No analogous right exists in U.S. law. Though parents and schools cannot be prohibited from teaching languages other than English, the state is simply not obligated to provide affirmative assistance in linguistic or cultural maintenance.

The negative liberty the U.S. Constitution affords is not trivial. It protects the rights of language minorities in the private sphere to maintain institutions such as foreign language presses, and to use non-English languages freely. These very basic rights have been denied language minorities around the world throughout history: the Kurds in Turkey and Catalan speakers in Franco's Spain are but two examples of groups whose languages have been banned altogether. But the right to preserve one's language remains largely a private right in the United States, one the state affirmatively supports only to the extent that language minorities win recognition of their linguistic interests through the political process.

The civil rights laws do provide some protection for those whose preference or natural inclination is to speak a language other than English. An Executive Order issue by President [Bill] Clinton and reaffirmed by President [George W.] Bush interpreted Title VI of the Civil Rights Act of 1964 to require all recipients of Federal funds to make their programs accessible to non-English speakers, and the Equal Employment Opportunity Commission has interpreted Title VII of the same Act to make English Only workplace rules presumptive violations of the law. States such as California and Illinois also have passed laws that restrain employers' authority to restrict the languages their employees may speak. These protections arguably enable language minorities to use and maintain their languages in the public sphere, and they require public entities to structure their institutions to make space for language minorities. But, as I explain later, most of these protections are transitional in nature, or intended to facilitate language minorities' move into the English speaking mainstream, not to recognize the right of linguistic minorities in and of themselves. . . .

Question: In your brief, you discuss institutions of civic life such as the courtroom, the classroom, the workplace and the administrative state. Would you discuss how giving students access to their own language is important to their participation in these spheres of civic life.

The benefits of being able to communicate in English . . . are substantial and well appreciated, the importance of staving off language loss is not.

We must begin from the premise that our linguistic profile is defined by what I call the mutability continuum of language. Even as the children and grandchildren of immigrants become native English speakers, the ongoing entrance of new immigrants will ensure that speech communities made up of non-English speaking immigrants, their English speaking descendants, and a range of bilinguals in between will continue to populate our society. Even the second and third generation descendants of immigrants, who will inevitably be English dominant, will retain ties to linguistically diverse speech communities. As a result, we have an interest in facilitating at least three types of communication: communication within linguistic minority communities; communication among individuals from different communities; and communication between subcommunities and the body politic generally. Language minority students growing up in the United States and being educated in our public schools are uniquely positioned to engage in each of these forms of communication, or to serve as the bilingual bridges that will help to keep our society woven together.

Finally, though the benefits of being able to communicate in English across groups and with the mainstream are substantial and well appreciated, the importance of staving off language loss is not. But children's loss of their capacity to speak a home language can have dramatic implications for family relations, introducing distance into the parent–child relationship and undermining the ability of parents to pass on values, skills, and advice. Language loss also separates children from the larger social networks that make up the world in which they reside. For many immigrant groups, affiliation with the minority community is crucial to the accumulation of social capital necessary for survival and social development in a new society. As new research on the phenomenon of so-called segmented assimilation is demonstrating, for some immigrant children, remaining closely connected to immigrant networks increases the chances of educational and economic success, because of the stability and community such closeness provides. Nurturing bilingualism fosters this connection and is thus essential to the successful adaptation and development of many immigrant students.

Language rights in the United States largely cease to exist once one has acquired English speaking ability.

Question: You state that "Courts have not understood the 'right' in question as a right to language, but as a right to the English language." Would you mind discussing that statement in more detail?

Language rights in the American context are transitional rights, or rights belonging to individuals unable to speak English. In contrast to the language rights protected under the Canadian constitution, which include the rights of French and English speakers to interact with the state in their mother tongue, language rights in the United States largely cease to exist once one has acquired English speaking ability.

In the context of bilingual education, for example, it is understood that children from language minority groups in the public schools have a civil rights interest in language instruction that promotes English language proficiency and overall academic achievement. The right is thus to an equal educational opportunity, not a right to maintain or preserve the mother tongue. With one outlying and dated exception, the Federal courts have never interpreted this civil rights imperative to require bilingual or bicultural education. Instead, they have required school districts to use their judgment about the best means to promote English language acquisition. Courts evaluate those judgments based on a three-part test. School must base their language instruction program on a legitimate educational theory recognized as sound. The program must be implemented effectively, and schools must devote resources and personnel to ensuring that the theory becomes reality. And the program must be evaluated after a trial period to ensure that the school does not persist in ineffective methods of instruction ([e.g.,] *Castañeda v. Pickard* [1978]). The touchstone for evaluation is success in promoting English language proficiency alongside academic achievement, which is measured through English language testing, not in terms of native language maintenance.

Federal and state statutes protect various other language rights, but as with the right to educational opportunity, they are rights intended to assist those in the process of learning English, not to protect the interests of language groups qua [as] language groups. Perhaps the most widely known and controversial example of this sort of transitional language right is the Voting Rights Act's requirement that jurisdictions whose language minority populations surpass a set threshold provide bilingual ballots and oral voting assistance during elections. This amendment was added to the Act in 1975 to address language minorities' effective exclusion from the polls, particularly in Texas, and was seen as compensation for the failure of the public schools to teach English adequately to language minorities. Bilingual ballots remain required by law today and are justified by the theory that all citizens, regardless of their linguistic abilities, should be able to participate in democracy. But they would no longer be necessary as a matter of law were English universally used.

In a similar vein, the importance of enabling participation by language minorities was recognized by President Clinton when he issued the Executive Order mentioned earlier. Pursuant to the order, law enforcement, healthcare providers, state and local governments, and all other recipients of Federal funds must therefore make a reasonable effort to provide for translation and interpretation of their services. This obligation is only triggered, however, when a fund recipient serves a community made up of a substantial number of limited English proficient individuals. In other words, bilingual services are contingent upon the existence of large communities of people unable to speak English; they do not attach to all language minorities.

It is inhumane to expect people to operate at all times in a language they do not understand or have not mastered.

The English Only Movement

To characterize language rights in the United States as instrumental rather than substantive is not to undermine their importance. The bread and butter of the English Only Movement is opposition to instrumental language rights, on the grounds that they slow assimilation. States and localities around the country have adopted official English laws, many of which would deny translated and interpreted services to non-English speakers.

Despite its popularity, the English Only approach obscures a crucial but under-appreciated fact: the process of learning English takes time. As a result, instrumental language rights are essential to the efficiency and openness of a democratic society, particularly in an era of high immigration. Though some English Only measures are motivated by understandable cost concerns, the outright refusal to provide even basic translation or interpretation presents public health and safety risks. Securing parental involvement in the schools also depends on schools having the capacity to reach out to and communicate with parents. Finally, it is inhumane to expect people to operate at all times in a language they do not understand or have not mastered, particularly during moments of emergency and great vulnerability. For those who are newly arrived in the United States, the world can seem inscrutable. Making institutions accessible invites people to engage them, leaving us all better off.

The desire among immigrants to learn English is insatiable. ESL [English as a Second Language] classes are oversubscribed, and to keep pace with current immigration trends, more classes are needed. But abandoning our commitment to instrumental language rights would only succeed in isolating precisely those whom we should be making the greatest effort to integrate into our society.

10

Multilingual Children Are Valuable Assets to Schools and Society

Marilyn Brown

Marilyn Brown is a reporter for the Tampa Tribune.

Hillsborough schools in Florida have more than 150 languages represented among their students. These multilingual students reflect a national trend among children who are preserving their native languages. Students report that they continue speaking their native language both to communicate with family members and because the perception about being multilingual is changing among their peers who are accepting of bilingualism. This trend will benefit the United States, particularly the military and the economic sectors, in the long run, as more Americans learn to speak the world's languages.

Official reports disguise Hillsborough [County, Fla.] schools' real diversity.

Ethnic categories are usually broad—black, white, Hispanic, Asian, Indian, multiracial.

It's the languages spoken at home that reveal how much of the globe the families of Hillsborough County represent.

"The languages are just mind-boggling," said Sandra Rosario, Hillsborough schools' supervisor of programs for English Language Learners. "They're a truer flavor of the cultures, the regions."

Marilyn Brown, "Tampa Bay Area Schools a Tapestry of Languages," *McClatchy-Tribune Regional News*, May 15, 2009. Reproduced by permission.

Students in Hillsborough schools spoke more than 150 foreign languages at home when their parents enrolled them.

The languages range from Abkhazian, spoken in the region between Russia and the Black Sea, to Zulu, an official language of South Africa. Nearly 31,000 students spoke Spanish at home; six of the 20 most commonly spoken languages are from India.

The focus has shifted from immigrants as a problem to immigrants as a resource.

A district tally shows nearly every school has students in the cultural mix. Most have students who speak an array of languages—many a dozen or more. Students at King High and Tampa Palms Elementary speak more than three dozen languages.

The numbers reflect a national trend.

The focus has shifted from immigrants as a problem to immigrants as a resource, said Joy Kreeft Peyton, vice president of the Washington [D.C.]-based Center for Applied Linguistics.

"After [the terrorist attacks of] Sept. 11, 2001, national security started to say, 'There are languages we need to know,'" Peyton said. "It is important for defense and commerce. These are big."

The importance of recognizing other languages and cultures is to affect "the way we view the world," she said. "To make the invisible visible . . . enriches us."

Difficulties Faced by English Learners at School

Some bilingual and trilingual students were born in the United States and picked up their families' native languages at home, but many arrive in this country with few, if any, English skills.

That made going to American schools difficult at first for Mohammed Hussein, a 17-year-old King High senior born in Jordan. He has been in the United States nearly five years but speaks mainly Arabic or Egyptian while working at his cousin's Green Land Middle Eastern restaurant near Temple Terrace.

"It was hard," he said.

Hussein said he got into fights early in his American education, when he was misunderstood, but that stopped when he became more proficient in English. He is learning Spanish from friends and television. He hopes to learn Spanish more quickly by living in the Dominican Republic for a year.

"I love Spanish," he said. "My grandmother is from Cuba. I love the language."

Students who speak very little English usually go through a "silent period," teachers said. They listen and won't speak until they are sure of their words, which can be isolating.

But many students describe being bilingual as "cool."

"Other people want to learn your language, too, because it sounds so cool," said Kimoanh Nguyen, 18, a Riverview High senior who was born in California and learned Vietnamese from his family.

Principals, teachers and students see the change in perception.

"All of the children are very curious about Chinese," said Kimberly Keenan, principal of Tampa Palms Elementary. "They see the symbols on their computer games."

Many children at Tampa Palms are from other countries and living in the Bay area while their parents attend the University of South Florida, Keenan said.

"It's amazing how they're able to retain their first language and culture," she said. "After their parents finish their education, many of them leave and go back to their country speaking English."

The Benefits Multilingual Children Bring to Education

The school benefits from the students' international culture, Keenan said.

"They add such a depth of experience. It teaches children lessons that aren't measured on the FCAT [Florida's Comprehensive Assessment Test]."

No one is certain how many Hillsborough students retain their native languages after they enroll in school and learn to speak English. But educators say those who enrolled in kindergarten and speak English through high school are likely to forget their native language unless parents make an extraordinary effort.

Such efforts have helped 9-year-old Spriha Shrestha remain adept at speaking Nepali. No one else at Dunbar Elementary Magnet School speaks the language, but she uses it daily with her relatives.

"Most of my class thinks it's cool that I am speaking this language," Spriha said. "They don't know anyone from Nepal."

Mandira Shrestha wants her daughter to also learn Newari, an ancient language still spoken in parts of Nepal that her family also speaks.

Rosario said she thinks Hillsborough schools don't know the total number of students who speak native languages at home because not all parents report it when they register kids for school.

Teachers and administrators also don't always know which students are bilingual.

"A lot of times I just stumble upon these kids as they come in the front door with their parents and they interpret for the parents," said Kathy Flanagan, principal at Smith Middle School near Citrus Park. Smith students speak 15 languages other than English, a typical number for Hillsborough schools.

Students and adults often assume those who appear Asian or Hispanic speak Chinese or Spanish.

That's not always true.

Katrine Hsiung speaks Indonesian, but her sons James, 13, and William, 14, speak only English. Their father, Edwin, is of Chinese descent but was born in the United States and speaks only English.

The boys were born in Tampa and spoke Indonesian at home with their mother and grandmother until they were in preschool.

Once the boys were in school, they did not want to respond in Indonesian anymore, Hsiung said. She regrets not encouraging the boys to speak Indonesian so they would "at least have more than one language. It's just knowledge."

James attends Smith and will travel to Indonesia this summer, hoping to pick up the language again.

"It's a good way to keep my own culture," he said.

William, who attends Hillsborough High's International Baccalaureate program, has friends who speak other languages and wishes he did, too.

It's better to speak more languages . . . you never know where a child's future is going to be.

"I would love to have that back," he said.

Of the 20 most popular languages used by Hillsborough students at home, six are spoken in India.

Kireet Agrawal, 12, attends Williams Middle Magnet School and speaks English fluently. He came to the United States from India with his parents when he was 4 months old. His father, Manish, who speaks four languages, required Kireet to speak Hindi at home.

"It's better to speak more languages," said his mother, Aradhana Agrawal. "The way the world is today going, you never know where a child's future is going to be."

11

English-Only Legislation Causes Problems for Public Libraries

Nicole M. Nicolino

Nicole M. Nicolino is a doctoral candidate at the University of Iowa College of Law.

English-only groups have endangered the ability of libraries to continue meeting the needs of the public they serve. In some communities, English-only laws have limited the ability of government workers to communicate to customers in their native language, and many believe that libraries likewise should not provide foreign-language collections. However, libraries with foreign-language collections often draw English-learners to their buildings where they can participate in programs such as English conversation groups. Libraries must retain the ability to provide educational materials in the languages spoken by their patrons. To limit such collections to English-language materials would violate their patrons' First Amendment rights.

At least forty-seven million people, or eighteen percent of those living in the United States, speak a language other than English at home. The two most commonly spoken languages in the home, other than English, are Spanish and Chinese. These numbers are increasing, but the reality of the United States as a multilingual society is not a new one, nor is it new that U.S. citizens and the government have expressed

Nicole M. Nicolino, "Por Que No Podemos Leer en la Biblioteca?: Questioning the Application of Official English Legislation to Public Libraries," *Journal of Gender, Race and Justice*, Spring 2007. Copyright © 2007 University of Iowa. Reproduced by permission.

concern about and opposition to a multilingual society. Groups advocating English as the official language of the United States are powerful lobbying forces that have achieved some success. Twenty-seven states now recognize English as their official language.

While no legislation has expressly forbidden foreign-language collections, libraries have drawn criticism for providing these materials.

English-Only Legislation and Libraries

The growing number of foreign-language speakers in the United States has increased the demand for information and literature in a variety of languages. Library collections often include books, magazines, and newspapers in foreign languages. Hundreds of libraries in at least forty states, including states with English as the official language, provide information in Spanish on their websites and on their shelves. The demand for foreign-language materials in public libraries has been high for several decades; for example, when Los Angeles' Chinatown Branch opened in 1977, all 500 Chinese-language books were checked out on the first day.

While no legislation has expressly forbidden foreign-language collections, libraries have drawn criticism for providing these materials. In Denver, Colorado, the public library system recently proposed seven "Language and Learning" branches to address the growing needs of its large Hispanic population. Denver, which is thirty-five percent Hispanic, also offers English conversation groups and Spanish-language G.E.D. [General Educational Development] courses at its public libraries. Such services are not limited to cities with large populations of language minorities. In Iowa City, Iowa, which is less than three percent Hispanic, the public library offers introductory internet classes for Spanish speakers as well as English conversation groups and other educational programs. . . .

According to the stated purposes and goals of federal funding statutes, libraries play an educational role in U.S. society and are intended to reach out to people from diverse ethnic and linguistic groups. The history and stated purpose of the American Library Association and librarians throughout the nation reinforce these goals. English-only legislation threatens the vital educational role that libraries play in society and violates the First Amendment rights of language minorities to receive foreign-language materials. . . .

Public Libraries Are Responsible to the Public

Libraries are obligated to act as an educational service for their patrons because they are federally funded as such. The Supreme Court has recognized parents' rights to direct their children's education, and it has declared that students have constitutional rights while at school. In disciplinary situations, the Court has balanced students' interests in education against those interests of teachers and school administrators in order and safety at the school. Public libraries, however, do not have the same interests as schools or teachers. In light of these different interests, discussed below, the freedom of individuals to direct their own educations and those of their children must be given even greater respect in a library situation. The following sections elaborate on the role of libraries and the varying educational interests involved.

> *English-only legislation might prohibit libraries from continuing to provide opportunities for language minorities to practice English and educate themselves.*

Librarians and the American Library Association (ALA) view themselves in light of their educational obligation, endorsing "comprehensive efforts to ensure that school, public, academic, and special libraries in every community cooperate to provide lifelong learning services to all." The ALA's goal of providing for lifelong learning is especially important to individuals learning English. These individuals arrive in the United States at varying ages and levels of formal education. Ignoring this group of learners when making acquisition choices would severely diminish the ability of a library to live up to its educational purpose.

A library can fulfill its educational obligations by combining traditional access to information with community outreach programs. Libraries function as meeting places for many community groups and offer classes about using computers and the internet, which provide practical education to low-income and elderly people who may not otherwise have an opportunity to build these skills. Some of these outreach programs require library resources, but many require nothing more than space and the foresight to organize a learning opportunity. An example of such a program is the Iowa City Public Library's English conversation group for non-native speakers. English-only legislation might prohibit libraries from continuing to provide opportunities for language minorities to practice English and educate themselves. Such an application of the law is counterintuitive because these services further the goal of English-language acquisition by providing low-cost opportunities to language minorities who wish to improve their English, a goal that English-only supporters share.

A Library's Interests Differ from a School's Interests

Schools are generally given wider latitude than other state actors when they decide to restrict the rights of students. A school's need for discipline and its obligation to educate students means that it has broad discretion when deciding upon curriculum and disciplinary policies. In contrast, a library's role is to provide varied information to a wide audience, so patrons may educate themselves. The librarian's role is more passive in relation to the individual library patron, while a teacher's role in a student's education is more active and affirmative. A librarian provides materials that eventually the library patron will access on his or her own, but a teacher must actively engage a child, relaying information personally.

The U.S. Supreme Court seemed to recognize this distinction in *Board of Education v. Pico*, where a school district removed nine books from the high school library. The school board had decided to remove the books on moral grounds, stating that they were "anti-American, anti-Christian, anti-sem[i]tic, and just plain filthy." Justice [William J.] Brennan [Jr.], writing for the plurality, drew a distinction between textbooks required in the classroom and books provided for voluntary reading in a school library. While schools generally have discretion in choosing curriculum and directing the learning of students, that discretion is more limited within the school library because of the self-directed nature of learning there. Pico's reasoning applies with even more force in the non-school library setting where there is no state interest in a particular type of learning; the goal is learning for its own sake. With these differences in mind, foreign-language materials do not implicate a library's efficiency and other interests the way a multilingual classroom might implicate a teacher's or school's interests. The state, acting through the library, deserves less latitude when it comes to limiting foreign-language materials because its interests are not as strong as they are within the school setting.

Libraries Should Provide Materials in the Community's Most Commonly Spoken Languages

Parents have a right and a duty to direct the education of their children. Several cases have dealt with this right in the context of language, beginning with the 1923 Supreme Court decision in *Meyer v. Nebraska*. In *Meyer*, the state of Nebraska prohibited teaching foreign languages to students in eighth grade or younger and prohibited any subject from being conducted in a foreign language. The statute applied to both public and private schools. This law was aimed at preventing children from learning the German language, as well as other modern languages, because they were seen as a threat to American values. The Meyer Court noted that "[u]nfortunate experiences during the late war and aversion toward every characteristic of truculent adversaries" made the motivation behind the law understandable. This statement seems to acknowledge and validate the prejudices that led to Nebraska's adoption of the law. Nevertheless, the Court invalidated the law because it interfered with the rights of teachers as well as parents to provide foreign-language instruction to children.

The goals of language discrimination are not accomplished by prohibiting libraries from holding foreign-language materials.

Because *Meyer* establishes that parents have a right to provide a foreign-language education to their children and that teachers have a right to teach a foreign language, the state should not be allowed to interfere with such a right unless its interests outweigh it. As explained above, the state's purported goal in passing English-only legislation is to promote English as the common language of the state and to increase incentives to learn English. In a library setting, this goal does not outweigh the rights of parents who want their children to learn or retain their native language. Even if English is used in the home, knowledge of the native language may be the only way a child can communicate with family members who do not speak English. Additionally, maintaining a foreign-language collection would not in any way decrease the ability of a library patron to use and learn from English-language materials.

Meyer should invalidate the application of English-only legislation to libraries because such legislation does the same thing the statute in *Meyer* did—it restricts the right of parents to direct the education of their children. The library exists simply to provide the materials necessary to educate oneself. A parent's right to direct the education of his or her child, coupled with the "passive" character of the librarian's obligation to educate, should allow for greater parental control of the child's language skills outside of the school. Children should have access to books not only in English but also in their native language or the native language of their family members and ethnic group.

Language Minorities Should Have a Right to Relay and Receive Information in their Native Language

Language should be considered a pure form of speech warranting the full protection of the First Amendment. Language discrimination, especially in public libraries, should be subject to strict scrutiny. The goals of language discrimination are not accomplished by prohibiting libraries from holding foreign-language materials. . . .

The First Amendment protects not only the right to free speech, but also the right to receive information. Even English-only advocates recognize that they cannot prohibit individuals from speaking non-English languages in their private lives. Despite this fact, there is no recognized right to speak one's native language. Some have even argued that one's language is not speech at all, but merely expressive conduct. The Ninth Circuit disagreed in *Yniguez v. Arizonans for Official English*, stating that "language is by definition speech, and the regulation of any language is the regulation of speech." Additionally, the court stated that "the decision to speak in another language is a decision involving speech alone." It further stated that even under a relaxed test for expressive conduct, Arizona's English-only statute would be unconstitutional. The Supreme Court vacated the Ninth Circuit's holding on grounds of mootness, but its reasoning is still important and persuasive.

Since English-only laws prohibit government employees from speaking or providing information in languages other than English, courts may defer more to government rationales for such prohibitions. "[I]t is the government's interest in performing its functions efficiently and effectively that underlies its right to exercise greater control over the speech of public employees." In the context of English-only laws, however, the speech of public employees is directly linked to the receipt of information by members of the public who seek their services. An English-only statute should not be given the same deference that other rules governing the speech of public employees are given because it also affects private individuals' rights to receive information under the First Amendment.

Even English-only advocates recognize that they cannot prohibit individuals from speaking non-English languages in their private lives.

English-Only Laws Are Too Restrictive

English-only laws restrict communication between the government and citizens. The proposed statute before Congress forbids official government activity in languages other than English with few exceptions. Knowledge of English would be a prerequisite to applying for driver's licenses and benefits as well as voting, barring a finding of unconstitutionality. An Arizona state senator, Jamie Gutierrez, attempted to join the *Yniguez* litigation as a plaintiff because he feared that speaking Spanish with his constituents would violate the state's English-only law. It would be alarming and highly inconsistent with

American principles of democracy to allow the exclusion of an entire group of people from proper government representation based on lack of English proficiency.

Some might argue that a library could easily carry an English translation of a foreign-language text, so the language minority is not kept from receiving the ideas or information sought. This argument is only applicable in situations where the language minority also speaks English and therefore has the ability to receive information in English. The argument also fails because it refuses to recognize language as more than a mere "middle man" through which individuals transmit information and ideas.

The fact that information can be translated from one language to another does not diminish a language minority's right to receive information in his or her native language. Language is a cultural construction that shapes how we view our world: "[i]t is not just a matter of remembering how to substitute a word from one language to that of another. Rather, it is a matter of learning a whole new way of processing thought, a different way of viewing the world." English-only advocates in the early twentieth century even used this argument to justify the prohibition on teaching German that gave rise to *Meyer*. In *Meyer*, the Supreme Court recognized this argument but held that a state may not prohibit foreign-language education to avoid the cultural enrichment that accompanies knowledge of a different language.

The translatability argument is even weaker in a library setting where many foreign-language materials are embodied in literature, not simply factual information that is easily translated. Literature cannot be translated as easily or as effectively as some other types of speech. Word choice and arrangement reflect choices by the author; in the discipline of literary analysis, how an author says something is often more important than what happens in the story. Colombian novelist Gabriel Garcia Marquez, who won the Nobel Prize in Literature in 1982, writes in his autobiography about the "bankrupt habit" of using words that end in "-mente," which is the Spanish equivalent to English "ly" adverbs. Marquez explains the importance of his decision to not use such words in his writing and expresses ignorance about whether translators of his novels stayed faithful to this aspect of his writings:

> I began to correct them whenever I ran across [words ending in—mente], and each time I became more convinced that this obsession was obliging me to find richer and more expressive forms. For a long time there have not been any in my books except for an occasional quotation. I do not know, of course, if my translators have detected and also acquired, for occupational reasons, this stylistic paranoia.

Marquez's situation illustrates not only the literary importance of word choice and grammar but also the potential for inaccurate or unfulfilling translations of literature, regardless of whether they are done in good faith. For these reasons, a library should be allowed to provide important literature in its native language when the community supporting the library speaks that language. . . .

Access to Foreign-Language Materials Is Beneficial to Society

As argued above, the presence of foreign-language materials might be the best way to draw non-English speakers to the library. They will be able to take part in English-learning activities at libraries because they will feel comfortable enough to spend time there. English speakers who desire to learn another language will also have access to reading materials that will improve their fluency.

If state governments are concerned about how to provide information efficiently to all people, libraries are ideal places to provide translations of important government documents. Several people will have access to the same paper copies, reducing printing costs to the government. This access will produce better-informed citizens by giving language minorities access to news articles, the internet, and government materials in their native languages. The result of this increased understanding will likely be less time and money spent on live translators elsewhere.

English-only advocates argue that learning English is the best way for immigrants to succeed economically in the United States. This does not necessarily require that the immigrant know only English. In today's global economy and diverse society, bilingualism is a valuable job skill. Education in general is important for any person's future success. Studies show that it takes several years to be proficient enough in a second language to work on an academic level. The best way to provide an education to a language minority is to allow that person to continue learning concepts and analysis skills in his or her native language while at the same time building English skills. Requiring students to wait until they are able to understand an academic concept in English that they could understand if taught in their native language would keep them constantly behind. By the time they reach the necessary proficiency level, it could be time to either go to college or get a job. If the student has never learned the analytical skills needed for college, he or she will have few options. Learning English will not have improved this individual's chances at economic success.

In the context of libraries . . . the justifications for English-only legislation do not exist.

Libraries are an accessible place for students and others to build analytical skills by reading in their native language. Some libraries have provided extra help to language minorities, making sure they are able to succeed in school while they learn a new language. A library branch in Long Beach, California set up an after-school program for Cambodian students to help them with their homework. The program helped nearly 900 students in one year, reducing drop-out rates among new immigrant children in the community. Even if a particular library is unable to provide bilingual staff and the extra help described above, easy access to foreign-language materials or even links to foreign-language websites can provide the information that a language minority needs.

English-only legislation should not be interpreted to bar public libraries from maintaining foreign-language materials. This interpretation would violate First Amendment and Equal Protection rights of language minorities. Classifications based on language deserve strict scrutiny because of the special link language has to national origin and the susceptibility of language classifications to hidden discriminatory goals. English-only laws do not further any state purpose when they are used to keep foreign-language books out of libraries. In the context of libraries, where the educational goal is not accompanied by the affirmative obligation to teach, the justifications for English-only legislation do not exist and sometimes can be turned on their heads.

12

Libraries Should Not Support Multiple Languages

Julia Stephens

Julia Stephens writes for American Libraries.

Libraries have a large role to play in the debate about immigration and the identity of America. Although libraries are pressured by lobbying groups and patrons to provide foreign language materials, doing so does a disservice to their Spanish-speaking populations who need to learn English to create a better life for themselves and their families. Libraries need to understand their importance in preserving the identity of America.

In light of the legal and illegal immigration waves of the last 20 years, libraries today face a number of controversies: Questions are swirling about language and library books, bilingual library websites, and English classes for immigrants—largely questions that concern outreach to Hispanic patrons and their right to materials in their native language. The discourse is especially heated when it comes to library policies concerning Spanish-language collection development, public services to illegal immigrants, and improvement of English skills in the Hispanic population.

Libraries and American Identity

In a framework that pits American pluralism against ethnocentrism, our founding principles of a unified nation with one language are being cast aside. All immigrants deserve access to public libraries, but when some lack the English-language skills necessary to read library books and journals, librarians have a choice: Change our American pluralistic philosophy to an ethnocentric one, or retain a "common American identity," as Arthur M. Schlesinger Jr. describes in *The Disuniting of America: Reflections on a Multicultural Society*: "A common language is an essential bond of cohesion in so heterogeneous a nation as America," he asserts. And I agree.

Libraries help maintain our American identity and unity as a nation when they stock books in our common language: Standard English. America's strength as a world power lies in this common language, which ties us together as a country and allies us with Britain, Ireland, Canada, Australia, and India. Our representatives in Congress agree: In May 2006, the Senate approved making English the official language of our nation. In a charged debate, they voted 63 to 34 to designate English as the national language.

Language as it relates to book selection is one issue under discussion in libraries today—an issue that, in the future, may be controlled by demographics. Ethnocentric librarians believe that libraries should reflect the diversity of community demographic ethnic groups. According to the Migration Policy Institute, Hispanics now make up 15% of our 300-million population, and some feel that library bookshelves should contain up to 15% Spanish-language fiction and nonfiction, depending on local demographic ratios.

The influx of illegal Hispanic immigrants over U.S. southwestern borders is currently estimated by the Pew Hispanic Center to be as much as 700,000 per year. Some American cities are experiencing an unprecedented amount of immigration to the point that there is now an outflow of population to smaller heartland cities. Librarians should be aware of the implications of this tidal wave of immigrants from Mexico and Central America over the last 20 years: America's libraries are being pressured to become bilingual on demand, but they are unprepared for the huge task of reaching out to the millions of both legal and illegal immigrants who are illiterate in English.

While libraries have a duty to offer all services to any patron, the rapidly changing demographics, largely due to illegal immigration, will affect the way libraries do business as the Hispanic minority inches toward a majority. Legal and illegal Spanish-speakers in the U.S. now number more than 40 million. Hispanic patrons want library websites in Spanish, programs for children in Spanish, and books in Spanish.

The unfunded White House Task Force on New Americans requires that all government agencies teach legal immigrants English. But an unfunded mandate means that local agencies will have trouble meeting this standard. Some libraries, however, are empowering legal immigrant patrons to use their collections by offering classes in English taught by volunteer literacy tutors.

Traditionally, new immigrants have been required to learn to speak English. Andrew Carnegie opened thousands of libraries in our country with the goals of providing books for the poor and helping immigrants to learn the language of the land, and, more to the point, the language that has become the dominant international language of commerce.

Bilingual Library Collections Do Not Help English Learners

Since the last major illegal-alien amnesty in 1986, the public school system has seen enormous growth in the demographics of immigration. Today, nearly one in five schoolchildren is Hispanic. Proficiency in English scores are below 30% for most 8th-graders. According to *The Nation's Report Card* for 2007, reading skills, though marginally improved, have not been accompanied by significant closing of ethnic gaps.

Even though public schools are required to accept all immigrants, some students are not literate in any language.

School libraries should offer these students English classes and Spanish books through interlibrary loan. Librarians and teachers are doing Spanish-speaking populations no favor by encouraging them to get by without learning English.

Multicultural groups who seek to divide the country into a bilingual society do not uphold America's ideals. School librarians' collection development policies are being affected by a Hispanic lobby, which includes library organizations such as the ALA [American Library Association] affiliate Reforma, an association that promotes library services to Latinos. Though this lobby pushes for bilingual libraries and dual-language schools, there is no evidence from test scores that bilingual programs increase English literacy.

Librarians should understand that it is by encouraging patrons to learn English that they open their collections to Hispanics and other immigrant groups.

School libraries can offer picture books for English learners, Latin American fiction in English, and multicultural nonfiction collections in English at middle and high school media centers. Multimedia CDs can help teach English. Grant programs are available to help build a library's Spanish-language collection without using limited school funds, which should be used to replace lost or worn books in English. Librarians in schools can teach information literacy in English to ESL [English as a Second Language] students. And school districts can offer after-school English classes for immigrant parents.

Many, if not most, taxpayers who support their local library did not support the immigration bill of 2007. Librarians need to become aware of local and state laws regarding providing public services to illegal immigrants. Immigrant-rights groups are lobbying library organizations for bilingual librarians and websites in Spanish. They want more Spanish collections of books and journals. A lack of funding and a lack of interest have stopped some libraries from replacing English books with Spanish, yet some libraries are buying as many as 1,000 books a year in Spanish. Libraries should not be weeding out books in English simply because multicultural or Hispanic groups request that they buy Spanish-language books.

Librarians should understand that it is by encouraging patrons to learn English that they open their collections to Hispanics and other immigrant groups. Websites and programs in English can encourage immigrant children to join the American culture and learn about the American experience.

When librarians build collections by community population ratios, they give in to ethnocentric demands for diversity equality with Spanish books and websites. The English-language culture that unites us disintegrates into an array of immigrant cultures.

By creating bilingual libraries, librarians are undermining the American democracy that has created one nation for all. Librarians have a duty to uphold the American way of life and save their English book and journal collections for Americans in the future.

13

Fear of Increased Immigration Has Led to Language Discrimination

Sandra Del Valle

Sandra Del Valle is a civil rights attorney and senior staff attorney at New York Lawyers for the Public Interest. She also is the author of Language Rights and the Law in the United States: Finding Our Voices.

The increase in immigration, particularly among Latino immigrants, is causing fear in some communities as long-term residents cope with the change that a new population brings. This fear is leading many to tie immigration and language together and push for laws that restrict minority languages or that require new immigrants to learn English. Language rights must be extended to protect those who speak minority languages.

In January of 2005, during a hearing on allegations of child abuse and neglect, Tennessee Judge Barry Tatum warned an 18-year-old mother originally from Oaxaca, Mexico to learn English or risk losing custody of her toddler daughter. The mother, Felipa Berrera, had been cited for neglect because of her failure to have her child immunized and for failure to keep 'appointments'. It is unclear from news articles whether the broken appointments were with the Department of

Sandra Del Valle, "The Bilingual's Hoarse Voice: Losing Rights in Two Languages," *Language Allegiances and Bilingualism in the United States.* Clevedon, U.K.: Multilingual Matters, 2009. Copyright © 2009 M. Rafael Salaberry and Sandra Del Valle. Reproduced by permission.

Children's Services or with a medical provider. It was the second order that he had issued within a year that linked child custody to a mother's ability to speak English. In his first decision, Judge Tatum had set a court date six months away during which he expected the mother of an 11-year-old to learn English at a fourth-grade level. The Court's order 'specifically informs the mother that if she does not make the effort to learn English, she is running the risk of losing any connection—legally, morally and physically—with her daughter forever'. In essence, Judge Tatum was prepared to terminate all parental rights, the most extreme punishment in child abuse cases, because of a mother's limited ability to speak English. His explanation for the order was that the mother ran 'the risk of losing out on all the opportunities' if she was not 'assimilated into our culture'. Judge Tatum's stated intention, then, was to help the mother and her children take advantage of US opportunities. Judge Tatum's orders and comments were warmly received by at least some of his neighbors. In her article, [reporter Ellen] Barry reported that one Tennessee resident stated that the immigrants had a 'moral obligation' to learn English. Then he added that if he were in Mexico he would 'make an effort to learn "Hispanic"'. A clerk at a local store commented that 'if you come through that door [indicating the store's front door] and you don't speak English, I'm sorry. If you love it that much here, you take the time to take an English class'.

The prevalence of Spanish on every Main Street . . . is used as a justification for the fear of an immigrant 'take over.'

Immigration and National Anxiety

Tennessee, like other southeastern states, has experienced a huge surge in its Latino population over the last ten years fueled by Mexican immigration to the state. Between 1990 and 2000, Tennessee's Latino population grew by 278%. These recent immigrants are predominantly young, male, poor and arriving directly from Mexico. This relatively noticeable homogeneity among recent arrivals makes their presence hard for small towns to ignore and can also seem overwhelming. Indeed, the growth of the Latino population in Tennessee is reflected throughout the country. From Chattahoochee, Georgia to Adams County, Pennsylvania, immigrants are no longer clustered into a few urban strongholds. The search for work has taken immigrants onto the tip of Long Island as well as the Deep South. National culture clash is occurring as long-time residents with little or no prior experience with immigrants meet very recently immigrated populations who, on their part, may only possess rudimentary or no English skills. For the native residents there is a growing anxiety that their known world is quickly becoming unknown.

The Texas custody cases exemplify a broader anxiety that, if left unchecked, immigrants may destabilize the nation; or, at the least, transform it beyond recognition. The proof, the anti-immigrants argue, is a perceived refusal on the part of immigrants to assimilate; the prevalence of Spanish on every Main Street in every corner deli, and in the 7-11 stores that dot busy intersections and wide streets is used as a justification for the fear of an immigrant 'take over'. Reactions throughout the nation have ranged from welcoming, to ambivalence to downright hostility. One small town after another has passed anti-immigrant laws or initiatives. Many times new laws are aimed at the young Mexican day laborers who came to the towns in search of work, many of which were undocumented and vulnerable to any number of hostile civic and political measures.

Immigration and Minority Languages

The laws and policies were clearly over-reaching but required expensive and time-consuming litigation in order to be stopped. For instance, the village of Mamaroneck, New York tried to criminalize standing on its sidewalks in the areas where the day laborers stood waiting for contractors to pick them up for work (although, in 2006 the policy was enjoined by a federal court as unconstitutional). Hazelton, Pennsylvania passed an ordinance prohibiting the rental of apartments to the undocumented. However, the Hazelton policy was challenged in court and enjoined in July 2007 in *Lozano et al. v. City of Hazelton*, No. 3:06 cv 1586. The town of Brookhaven on Long Island adopted a policy aimed exclusively at day laborers who rented illegal rooms in private houses. Rather than follow a legal process against the homeowners, the town sent its housing code enforcers to throw the men out of their homes in the middle of the night. Some men had to take shelter in the surrounding woods. Nevertheless, the town of Brookhaven was sued and, in October 2005, Judge Seybert, a federal district court judge, granted the plaintiffs an injunction prohibiting the town from continuing this policy.

The treatment of minority languages, whether historical or current, cannot be excised from the immigration debate.

The treatment of minority languages, whether historical or current, cannot be excised from the immigration debate. Those who use minority languages most visibly are the recent immigrants. If the immigrants are abhorred, derided or mistrusted, so too are their languages. In practical, social and political terms, immigrants and their languages are one and the same. If immigration and language are two strands of the same braid then the nationalism is certainly the last strand. Appeals to the nation's sense of pride and sacrifice—the attitude that 'America is for Americans' could not have been more sympathetically received than after 9/11 [2001 terrorist attacks]. The world grew uncomfortably smaller for the US after the bombing of the World Trade Center. The US, a country of unparalleled wealth and military might, had been taken by surprise by a small band of terrorists who could claim no country as their own. The nation was drawn together, but not in a kind of positive unity where its diversity was praised as a source of strength, but in fear, where diversity became suspect, even intolerable. Even though neither Mexico nor Mexican immigrants were even remotely involved with the terrorist attacks or terrorism, suspicion of the foreign born was pervasive. Soon after, there were calls for then-President [George W.] Bush to close the border with Mexico by literally building a wall. Pressured by Republicans, however, President Bush signed a bill authorizing the building of the wall even though it went against his own policies on immigration.

Since 9/11 the country has been in deep psychological turmoil, gripped by a 'loss of confidence' once used to describe the nation during World War I. A loss of confidence in the ability of the nation generally to sustain itself; to provide for the safety and well being of its citizens in the face of external, menacing factors. Anxiety that the nation will fail in its basic protective functions, turns inward as hostility toward anyone perceived as an outsider. Consequently, nationalism climbs to a hysterical pitch where 'the stranger' is perceived as 'menac-[ing] the unity, and therefore, the integrity and survival of the nation itself.'

There is a strong perception that the new immigrants simply do not want to assimilate and that they refuse to learn English.

Viewing Immigration in a Historical Context

There is an important mythology surrounding this country's immigrant history that shapes current political and judicial thinking. Today's immigrants and the language issues they raise are viewed and judged against the backdrop of the accepted but distorted national mis-history of the nation's earliest immigrants. Immigrants of the past are viewed through three inter-related modalities—refractions of light through one prism: (1) immigrants as the historical backbone of the country: the true and literal builders of the nation; (2) immigrants as historical representatives of a John Wayne-like rugged individualism who pull themselves up by their own bootstraps; (3) the US as a country which supports and allows for such success for those who are strong enough to grasp it. Essentially, immigrants became the receptacles for the nation's self-image: like a mirror, if the immigrant looked good, then so did the country. And the country was successful, economically burgeoning and, while immigrant friendly, was also confidently assimilative.

What was to be made then of today's immigrants landing on the nation's shores and through its southernmost deserts in a time of economic and military uncertainty? With the history of US immigration seen through such rosy glasses, there could only be one response: the differences between today's immigrants and yesterday's lays in the nature of the immigrants themselves. The lesson to be learned, argue today's anti-immigrants, is that the US need not change in reaction to large scale immigration because success for all has lain in the willingness of the immigrants to happily or at least willingly accommodate themselves to their new country. It is the immigrant who must change and model himself after the immigrants of the past as reinterpreted by the US majority. The further away the past, the more likely it will be distorted for present purposes. So that in the 1940s, General [George S.] Patton idolized the immigrant parents of his soldiers, the same people that were excoriated when they actually arrived thirty years earlier. While Patton considered immigrants to be noble souls, tugged toward the US because of its opportunities and helping to form its strong American character, Edward Ross, a social scientist writing in 1914, thought immigrants were 'hirsute, low-browed, big-faced persons of obviously low mentality.' It is through the lens of morality that the immigrants are judged, whether positively or negatively.

English-only policies and laws are touted as the harsh but necessary medicine.

Immigration and English-Only Policies

Today, there is a strong perception that the new immigrants simply do not want to assimilate and that they refuse to learn English. This refusal is seen either as patently disloyal as a consequence of continued loyalties to another country, or as a snub to US values and language. Either way the national culture would seem to be under siege as never before. The anti-immigration group, Federation for American Immigration Reform (FAIR) provides a national forum for this perspective. Its website (www.fairus.org) quotes diverse sources for its position that ethnic strife begins with language issues. FAIR equates today's Latino communities with the secessionists in Quebec. According to FAIR what they 'have in common is a determination to preserve a way of life. Dominant languages [here English] seem a threat to that, a challenge to family, church, and historical memory, and so they are resisted . . . .' There is an implicit paternalism here: that since 'Hispanic-American communities' feel most comfortable in the unscientific, instinctive, arguably less disciplined realms of 'family, church and memory', they do not belong and could not be successful in the US, a modern, innovative, forward-thinking country. Although FAIR would like to slow the trickle of immigration, for those less drastic, FAIR provides a rationale for approaching immigrants from another perspective. The immigrant, FAIR would argue, can be 'de-clawed', tamed, re-imagined as a friendly neighbor through US re-education;

perfect subjects for 21st century *noblesse oblige* [benevolent behavior considered to be the responsibility of persons of high birth or rank].

Deliberately or not, Judge Tatum's order for the Mexican mother to learn English efficiently carried a powerful parcel of images no US native would fail to understand. He wrapped the historical immigrant mythology, nationalism, and an un-differentiated anxiety, then sealed it with the missionary's self-righteousness: the immigrant must learn English quickly be-cause it is in her best interest. His response to the 'recalcitrant' immigrant is not only emotionally powerful but is at least os-tensibly unselfish: the push to learn English is for the immigrants' own good. In Judge Tatum's view, the immigrant is a lazy child who should not be coddled through minority language assistance. Instead, English-only policies and laws are touted as the harsh but necessary medicine. . . .

Language Rights

There is clearly much work to be done on achieving full lan-guage rights for minority languages in the US. The link be-tween immigration and minority language usage has in the past, played along more negative lines than positive ones. While bilingualism is generally perceived as a positive for the nation, those most likely to carry that vision forward, immi-grants, have also been the most maligned for the use of their native languages. There is a deep fear in the nation that the latest immigrants will not assimilate, and consequently, an in-tolerance even for bilingualism at least when exercised by new immigrants. The judiciary, reflecting this national anxiety, has been ambivalent about extending the traditional civil rights structure to include the more complex, ambiguous issues raised by language minorities.

Those issues include the covert forms of racism practiced by employers and public agencies, alike; the inter-marriage be-tween those of different races having multi-racial children, who do not fall into a neat racial category but may experience different, and so far, unacknowledged forms of racism; the socio-economic discrimination that plagues most minorities but White majorities as well. Whether there is room in the current civil rights paradigm for the resolution of these complex issues is yet to be seen. But the concerns raised about the legal treatment of language minorities, touches on all these issues. This has placed them on the cutting edge of what can be a new generation of civil rights jurisprudence. A place that is challenging, exciting and, like all cutting edges, risky.

Organizations to Contact

The editors have compiled the following list of organizations concerned with the issues debated in this book. The descriptions are derived from materials provided by the organizations. All have publications or information available for interested readers. The list was compiled on the date of publication of the present volume; names, addresses, phone and fax numbers, and e-mail and Internet addresses may change. Be aware that many organizations take several weeks or longer to respond to inquiries, so allow as much time as possible.

American Council on the Teaching of Foreign Languages (ACTFL)

1001 N Fairfax St., Suite 200, Alexandria, VA   22314
(703) 894-2900 • fax: (703) 894-2905
e-mail: headquarters@actfl.org
website: www.actfl.org

The American Council on the Teaching of Foreign Languages is a national organization focused on the improvement and expansion of language instruction. Some of its projects include the creation of language proficiency guidelines and New Visions in Action, a cooperative effort with the National K-12 Foreign Language Resource Center seeking to support language proficiency for all students. ACTFL publications include *Foreign Language Annals* and *The Language Educator*. The organization's website contains many documents about foreign language standards and other educational resources along with news briefs and access to an online community with blogs and discussion pages.

Center for Applied Linguistics (CAL)

4646 40th St. NW, Washington, DC   20016-1859
(202) 362-0700 • fax: (202) 362-3740

e-mail: info@cal.org
website: www.cal.org

The Center for Applied Linguistics provides a wide range of information, tools, and resources in an effort to improve communication through better understanding of language and culture. CAL's researchers and educators conduct research, design and develop instructional materials and language tests, provide technical assistance and professional development, conduct needs assessments and program evaluations, and disseminate information and resources related to language and culture. In addition to its newsletter, *CALnews*, the website includes an archive of the former print newsletter *Linguistic Reporter*, information about research and projects, downloadable digests, informational brochures, and numerous other publications. CAL also maintains databases and directories, such as the *Directory of Foreign Language Immersion Programs in U.S. Schools* and the *Online Directory of ESL Resources*.

Center for Multilingual, Multicultural Research (CMMR)
University of Southern California, Rossier School of Education, Waite Phillips Hall, Suite 604,
Los Angeles, CA 90089-0031
e-mail: rbaca@usc.edu
website: www.usc.edu/dept/education/CMMR/

The Center for Multilingual, Multicultural Research, a research unit at the University of Southern California, facilitates the research, collaboration, dissemination, and professional development activities of faculty, students, and others across the School of Education, the university community, and outside organizations. CMMR's website contains news items, information about current projects and current language policy and rights, a list of other professional organizations, and an index of full text articles, newspapers, and periodicals.

English First
8001 Forbes Pl., Suite 102, Springfield, VA 22151
(703) 321-8818 • fax: (703) 321-7636

website: www.englishfirst.org

English First is a national, nonprofit lobbying organization founded with the goals of making English America's official language, helping children learn English, and eliminating multilingual policies it believes are costly and ineffective. Information about current legislative efforts, a monthly newsletter, and numerous articles and press releases are available on the organization's website.

Institute for Language and Education Policy
PO Box 19025, Portland, OR   97280
e-mail: bilingualed@starpower.net
website: www.elladvocates.org/

The Institute for Language and Education Policy is a nonprofit organization working to promote research-based policies in serving English and heritage language learners. Toward that end, its website includes issue briefs, policy analysis, recent periodical articles, news bulletins, commentary articles, and public forums on various issues, including the No Child Left Behind Act, the English-only movement, and bilingual and heritage language education.

Linguistic Society of America (LSA)
1325 18th St. NW, Suite 211, Washington, DC   20036
(202) 835-1714 • fax: (202) 835-1717
e-mail: lsa@lsadc.org
website: www.lsadc.org

The Linguistic Society of America is committed to the advancement of the scientific study of language. To that end, LSA supports and distributes research, advocates for educational and political policies, and provides information to educate both officials and the public about language. The LSA has issued statements and resolutions on matters such as language rights, the English-only movement, and bilingual education, and the organization is a strong proponent of the documentation and revitalization of endangered languages both within the United States and abroad. Its website includes information about its annual meetings, publications, information on jobs in the field of linguistics, student resources, and an archive of its publication, *LSA Bulletin*.

National Association for Bilingual Education (NABE)

8701 Georgia Ave., Silver Spring, MD   20910
(202) 898-1829 • fax: (202) 789-2866
website: www.nabe.org

The mission of the National Association for Bilingual Education is to advocate for bilingual and English language learners and families and to cultivate a multilingual, multicultural society. NABE publishes the *NABE News and Bilingual Research Journal* as well as other publications with many back issues available online.

National Clearinghouse for English Language Acquisition (NCELA)

2011 Eye St. NW, Suite 300, Washington, DC   20006
(800) 321-6223 • fax: (800) 531-9347
e-mail: askncela@gwu.edu
website: www.ncela.gwu.edu

The National Clearinghouse for English Language Acquisition collects, coordinates, and conveys a broad range of research and resources in support of an inclusive approach to high-quality education for English-language learners. Authorized under Title III of the No Child Left Behind Act of 2001, the NCELA supports the U.S. Department of Education's Office of English Language Acquisition, Language Enhancement, and Academic Achievement for Limited English Proficient Students. NCELA's online resource library has numerous documents concerning English language education as well as state-by-state information on demographics, standards, assessments, and information on federal grants and funding. NCELA also publishes *AccELLerate!*, a quarterly newsletter covering issues of interest to stakeholders in education for English-language learners.

ProEnglish

1601 N Kent St., Suite 1100, Arlington, VA   22209
(703) 816-8821 • fax: (703) 527-2813
e-mail: mail@proenglish.org
website: www.proenglish.org

ProEnglish is a national, nonprofit organization working to make English the official language of the United States. ProEnglish specializes in providing legal assistance to public and private agencies facing litigation or regulatory actions associated with language. Its website contains educational materials and recent updates on language-related legislation.

Second Language Research Institute of Canada

PO Box/CP 4400,
Fredericton, NB E3B 5A3
Canada
(506) 453-5136 • fax: (506) 453-4777
e-mail: slec@unb.ca
website: www.unbf.ca/L2/

The Second Language Research Institute of Canada works to support second language education in Canada and abroad through teacher preparation, research, bilingual program evaluation, and policy development. The organization's website contains information on current language issues, available programs, teaching resources, and links to partner websites.

Teachers of English to Speakers of Other Languages (TESOL)

1925 Ballenger Ave., Suite 550, Alexandria, Virginia   22314
(703) 836-0774 • fax: (703) 836-7864
e-mail: info@tesol.org
website: www.tesol.org

The mission of Teachers of English to Speakers of Other Languages is to develop and maintain professional expertise in English language teaching and learning for speakers of other languages worldwide. TESOL publications are resources for teachers working with learners of English as an additional language and include the serials *TESOL Journal, TESOL Quarterly*, and a full catalog of books. TESOL also hosts an annual convention, and its website contains a news section as well as career resources.

U.S. Department of Education, Office of English Language Acquisition (OELA)

400 Maryland Ave. SW, Washington, DC   20202
website: www2.ed.gov/programs/sfgp/

The U.S. Department of Education's Office of English Language Acquisition provides national leadership under Title III and Title V of the No Child Left Behind Act to help ensure English-language learners and immigrant students attain English proficiency. OELA also helps to build the nation's capacity in critical foreign languages. OELA's website includes information about its services, special programs, initiatives, activities, and resources available to educators, parents, and students.

U.S. English Foundation

1747 Pennsylvania Ave. NW, Suite 1050,
Washington, DC   20006
(202) 833-0100 • fax: (202) 833-0108
website: www.usefoundation.org

The U.S. English Foundation contends that learning English quickly and learning it with English-speaking peers is the best way for English learners to get ahead academically and socially. The organization disseminates information about English teaching methods, sponsors educational programs, develops English instructional materials, represents the interests of official English advocates before state and federal courts, and promotes opportunities for people living in the United States to learn English. The U.S. English Foundation is a separate organization from U.S. English, Inc., which works to pass legislation related to the English language. The website contains a newsletter, information on current research and programs, and a listing of free online English-language learning resources.

U.S. English, Inc.
1747 Pennsylvania Ave. NW, Suite 1050,
Washington, DC   20006
(202) 833-0100 • fax: (202) 833-0108
website: www.us-english.org

U.S. English, Inc., is a citizens' action group working to preserve English as the official language of the United States through legislation. The website contains a news section with current information about national language efforts in addition to blogs, press releases, and other information about current legislation.

Bibliography

Books

Colin Baker

Foundations of Bilingual Education and Bilingualism. Bristol, UK: Multilingual Matters, 2006.

Maria Estela Brisk

Bilingual Education: From Compensatory to Quality Schooling, 2nd Ed. Mahwah, NJ: Lawrence Erlbaum Associates, 2006.

Stephen J. Caldas

Raising Bilingual-Biliterate Children in Monolingual Cultures. Bristol, UK: Multilingual Matters, 2006.

James Crawford

English Learners in American Classrooms: 101 Questions, 101 Answers. New York: Scholastic, 2007.

Tara Williams Fortune and Diane J. Tedick, eds.

Pathways to Multilingualism: Evolving Perspectives on Immersion Education. Bristol, UK: Multilingual Matters, 2008.

Patricia Gandara and Frances Contreras

The Latino Education Crisis: The Consequences of Failed Social Policies. Cambridge, MA: Harvard University Press, 2010.

Ofelia Garcia

Bilingual Education in the 21st Century: A Global Perspective. Malden, MA: Wiley-Blackwell, 2008.

Francois Grosjean   *Bilingual: Life and Reality.* Cambridge, MA: Harvard University Press, 2010.

Beth Harry and   *Why Are So Many Minority Students* Janette Klingner   *in Special Education?: Understanding Race and Disability in Schools.* New York: Teachers College Press, 2005.

Terry A. Osborn,   *Language and Cultural Diversity in* ed.   *U.S. Schools: Democratic Principles in Action.* Lanham, MD: Rowman & Littlefield Education, 2007.

Aneta Pavlenko,   *Bilingual Minds: Emotional* ed.   *Experience, Expression, and Representation.* Bristol, UK: Multilingual Matters, 2006.

Kim Potowski   *Language and Identity in a Dual Immersion School.* Bristol, UK: Multilingual Matters, 2007.

Jon Allan Reyhner   *Education and Language Restoration.* Philadelphia, PA: Chelsea House, 2006.

Periodicals

Tal Abbady   "Boca Raton Resident Seeks to Make English Official Language: Boca Raton Resident Heads Group Behind Official English Movement," *South Florida Sun-Sentinel*, October 8, 2007.

Carly S.
Americam

"This Is America: We Speak English and Nothing Is for Free," *People's Voice*, May 2006.

Robbie Brown

"In Nashville, a Ballot Measure That May Quiet All but English," *New York Times*, January 11, 2009.

———

"Language Barriers: English Has Never Been America's 'Official' Language. What's Behind the Recent Efforts to Change That?" *New York Times Upfront*, March 16, 2009.

Andrew Sangpil Byon

"Language Socialization in Korean-as-a-Foreign-Language Classrooms," *Bilingual Research Journal*, Summer 2006.

Cathy Coulter and Mary Lee Smith

"English Language Learners in a Comprehensive High School," *Bilingual Research Journal*, Summer 2006.

James Crawford and Edward Tabet

"A Disaster in Any Language," *Salem Statesmen*, October 29, 2008.

Carrie Peyton Dahlberg

"In Study, Bilingual Brains Stay Sharp Longer," *Sacramento Bee*, February 7, 2007.

Tony Dokoupil

"Why 'English Only' Will Get the OK in Oklahoma," *Newsweek*, May 31, 2010.

Adam Feller

"English Language Debate Renews Questions," *Associated Press*, May 20, 2006.

Henry Fountain   "In Language Bill, the Language
                        Counts," *New York Times*, May 21,
                        2006.

Eugene E. Garcia   "Helping Young Hispanic Learners,"
and Bryant Jensen   *Educational Leadership*, March 2007.

Richard Gartner   "Bilingual Pupils Do Better in
                        Exams, Study Finds," *The
                        Independent*, October 31, 2006.

Michael A. Kahn   "Make English the Official Language?
                        How About Just Learning to Use It
                        Correctly?" *St. Louis Post-Dispatch*,
                        June 2, 2008.

Jin Sook Lee and   "'It's Not My Job': K-12 Teacher
Eva Oxelson   Attitudes Toward Students' Heritage
                        Language Maintenance," *Bilingual
                        Research Journal*, 2006.

Kate Menken   "Teaching to the Test: How No Child
                        Left Behind Impacts Language Policy,
                        Curriculum, and Instruction for
                        English Language Learners," *Bilingual
                        Research Journal*, Summer 2006.

Doug Moore   "English Only?" *St. Louis
                        Post-Dispatch*, October 21, 2008.

Jay Nordlinger   "Bassackwards: Construction Spanish
                        and Other Signs of the Times,"
                        National Review, January 29, 2007.

Leonard Pitts Jr.   "It's Liberty, Not Language, That
                        Unites a Nation," *Miami Herald*, May
                        22, 2006.

Mary Jo Pitzl   "'Official English' Wouldn't Alter
                       Much," *Arizona Republic*, October 27,
                       2006.

Victor Manuel   "Immigrants Make English a
Ramos   Priority," *South Florida Sun-Sentinel*,
                       May 30, 2006.

Judith Rance   "Creating Intentional Communities
Rooney   to Support English Language
                       Learners in the Classroom," *English
                       Journal*, May 2008.

Diane Smith   "A One-*Dos* Punch," *Fort Worth
                       Star-Telegram*, April 10, 2007.

Elise Wattendorf   "Images of the Multilingual Brain:
and Julia Festman   The Effect of Age on Second
                       Language Acquisition," *Annual
                       Review of Applied Linguistics*, 2008.

Michelle R. Wood   "ESL and Bilingual Education as a
                       Proxy for Racial and Ethnic
                       Segregation in U.S. Public Schools,"
                       Journal of Gender, Race and Justice,
                       Spring 2008.

Index